2 ℓ³

A MANUAL FOR REMEDIAL READING

A MANUAL FOR REMEDIAL READING

BY

EDWARD WILLIAM DOLCH, Ph.D.

Assistant Professor of Education
University of Illinois

PUBLISHED IN CHAMPAIGN, ILLINOIS, BY
THE GARRARD PRESS
IN THE YEAR 1939

iv

PREFACE

Reading is now recognized as the chief tool for securing education, in school or out. In a country where we wish each individual to secure all the education of which he is capable, we therefore wish each individual to be as skillful a reader as possible. Thus each child's progress in reading becomes an important concern of the school at all grade levels. Reading tests have been devised for all grades, from first grade through college, and these tests are being used ever more widely to determine if we are actually making each individual so skillful a reader that he may take full advantage of the educational opportunities of reading matter, in school and outside of school.

Unfortunately, the results from the administering of reading tests are not too reassuring. It is very common to find, among children of any particular grade, reading abilities which cover a range of five or more grades. That is, children may be reading at a level two or more grades ahead of their grade while other children are reading at a level two or three years behind their grade. We are glad for the advanced readers, but are rather appalled by the number of retarded ones. It has been authoritatively stated that from one-fourth to one-third of children in our schools are retarded readers, and therefore are unable profitably to use their textbooks and equally unable profitably to use other reading matter to further their education.

Retarded readers are of two types. There are those, the great majority, who can be taken care of by the classroom teacher or by a special teacher who has given some study to remedial reading. There are also the few whose difficulties are so complicated that they must be studied and helped by a reading clinic. This book deals with the first and larger group. For that group, it gives methods of diagnosis and analysis. It also gives proven methods for the help of the retarded reader at each grade level. The problem is reteaching reading, but reteaching it this time so that it will quickly and surely be learned. All of the common types of cases are described and methods for successfully handling them are given. Any teacher can follow these methods with great success. Of course there will occasionally occur the other type of retarded reader, the complicated case that requires a reading clinic, but it will do no harm to that case to attempt the methods that work with most children. If these methods fail, there will be time to get further expert advice.

We wish to make it very clear that we are not presenting in this book a statement of the procedure of a reading clinic. Such a clinic contains workers of highly specialized training. It is supplied with special instruments for testing and training. It is prepared to deal with the strange and unusual cases that occasionally appear. It seeks to investigate problems as well as to give service. Teachers and administrators should use the services of reading clinics as far as possible. Complex cases and such as resist ordinary efforts should be taken to reading clinics. The vast majority of poor readers, however, can be given attention and help in the regular school. This book deals with that attention and help.

E. W. DOLCH.

Urbana, Illinois.

CONTENTS

CHAPTER I

POOR READING AND PERSONALITY

I. Each deficient reader is a personality problem.

Failure to learn to read as others do is a major catastrophe in a child's life. The child's failure is known to his family and to all his playmates. Even if teachers and parents try to save the child from the consequences of this failure, the situation is bad enough, because other children will certainly taunt the child with his inability to do something which they can do. Even if the teacher tries to be considerate, most parents will not be. They mistakenly think that scoldings and punishment will get desirable results. Even some teachers are guilty of making the life of the poor reader more unhappy by punishments and ridicule. These circumstances inevitably make their mark on a child's personality. They do this in even the first year of failure in reading, and if this failure continues for three or four years, the warping of personality becomes serious indeed.

All work in remedial reading must deal with the personality difficulties that poor reading has caused. This must be done, first of all, because the chief purpose of education is to develop future citizens with wholesome personalities. But we do this, in the second place, because it is found that success in remedial reading is generally dependent upon correction of the maladjustments that poor reading has produced. This fact will become clear as we discuss the major personality problems involved.

The capable, understanding teacher is the chief factor in correcting any personality difficulty. Such a teacher instinctively senses the child's problem in all its keenness. The child feels perfectly at ease with her, and frankly tells all his troubles. He knows that she is not going to "tell on him" or in any way betray any of his confidences. Thus she may in a very short time get to the bottom of a situation that school records or test scores do not seem to explain. Such a teacher meets the child as a friend or pal, but without losing her prestige as a wiser adult. Some children have learned to be suspicious of all adults and will respond more slowly than others. The teacher may take such a child on a trip, let him visit her home or otherwise have common experiences with him. Thus, the barrier may be broken down and real contact made. This contact is necessary if personality adjustments are to be made.

A. The child may believe that he is "too dumb" to learn to read.

Many children who have failed in reading are convinced that they cannot learn to read. Members of their family, playmates, and even teachers may have been telling them that their failure shows that they are "dumb." Few children have sufficient self-confidence to stand out indefinitely against this sort of pressure. The natural thing is to accept the verdict of others and therefore to quit trying. Many children thus go on, year after year, when with any real effort they might overcome their difficulty.

Unfortunately the effect of this conviction of being "dumb" is likely to spread to other fields also. If the pupil cannot learn to read, he may think he cannot learn to do other school work either. If he cannot do things in school, he may cease to expect to succeed in things outside of school. Failure in reading is likely to lead to a general sense of inferiority that will cripple the individual's whole life. One of the greatest compensations in remedial reading work is to see the transformation in a child when you have shown him, in spite of his conviction, that he *can* read.

B. The failure in reading may have developed marked lassitude and inertia.

A normal healthy child is active. There are many things he wants to do; and he wants to be doing something all of the time. The failure in reading often seems to have had all of this "desire to do" taken out of him. He may have become a mere "sitter" in the class room. He is surrounded with books out of which he can get nothing. Physical activity is prohibited, and mental activity without reading is difficult. After a year or two of this condition, there may develop a habit of indifference that may seem to resist all efforts to arouse interest or attention. Such a habit will block all learning and self-development. It produces a negative personality with which the school can often do little or nothing. Even a sense of inferiority is easier to overcome than this state of inertia and defeatism. The teacher's first task is to overcome this inertia by discovering some "spring" of interest and developing it. She may often have to do this entirely apart from all reading.

C. The child may be proud of being a non-reader.

Every individual craves distinction of some kind, and being the "pupil who can't learn to read" satisfies this craving on the part of some young children. We usually appeal to children to do things because other children do them and thus make use of the desire to be like others. But here is a child who does not want to be like others. He will resist efforts to teach him reading because if he learned how to read he would lose his distinction. This attitude is a great handicap to remedial reading work, but it is also a general personality problem. A child who discovers he can get attention by refusing to do the customary thing is likely to continue this process with disastrous results. Sometimes it is possible to convince the child who has taken this attitude that it is more fun to read than not to read. If he cannot be so convinced, we have to wait until the child is older and realizes how foolish he has been. When he reaches the middle grades and finds himself faced with failure because of non-reading, his desire for this kind of distinction usually disappears.

A similar situation sometimes arises when a non-reader is given special attention or privileges such as tutoring or excuse from regular classes. The child may want to retain these privileges and the distinction they may convey. His attention can, however, be secured by interesting materials, and he will learn to read even though he does not especially want to.

D. The failure in reading may have developed compensations elsewhere.

A frequent result of failure to learn to read is that the child merely ignores reading and puts all his interest and attention elsewhere. He may become especially good in some other school subject. He may get his satisfaction from art or music or similar special activity. He may develop a hobby. Or he may receive sufficient satisfaction from leadership in play. That leadership often means leadership in mischief. Truants and delinquents are often found to be non-readers, and their misconduct can often be traced to desire for "compensation."

A child of this type may seem entirely self-satisfied and normal, but we cannot regard him so because he actually carries with him a sense of failure even though he seems to have found happiness in spite of it. It is often said that we need not worry so much about this child's personality problem for he has done just what so many adults must do; he has found satisfaction in his abilities and ignored his weaknesses. Yet we must realize that, if the child is intelligent, disaster awaits him. He will be required to go on in school work, and sooner or later he will find it absolutely impossible to ignore his deficiency in reading. Therefore this child needs just as serious attention as any other type.

The child who has found his satisfactions outside of reading presents a type of indifference to remedial measures that is very hard to handle. Through friendship, the teacher must get him to tolerate the work. Then through hobbies or other interests she can get his increased attention. But above all, she must see that he actually learns to read. Success is the best remedy.

E. Remedial reading cases usually hate books.

Children who have failed in reading usually hate books or anything connected with books. It is hard for a teacher or in fact for any educated person to realize this. The only way to do so is to gain the full confidence of the children who have failed in reading and then get frank expressions from them. Such a strong feeling of antagonism toward the reading matter that is such an attraction to most of us is a serious personality distortion. It cuts the child off from the chief appeal of the school and the chief avenue of education. Until this emotional twist is corrected, little can be done to remedy the situation.

Methods of making contact with these cases are similar to those used with other types of disinterest or discouragement. Later, on page 53, an approach without use of books is described.

F. Failure in reading may have produced an attitude of non-coöperation with the school, if not positive antagonism toward it.

All too often, the remedial reading case "hates school." Thus a tremendous barrier is set up before our every effort. A teacher is disliked just because she is a teacher. All requests are refused because they emanate from the school. Regular attendance is not forthcoming. Nothing is done as requested. Such a situation is bound to exist if, for years, the child has been held up to ridicule and has had his self-respect attacked in every way by the school machinery. The revolt is in fact a sign of some character and strength of personality. Remedial reading with such a case is difficult indeed. It cannot begin as remedial reading at all. Instead, personal contact must be made through some avenue not connected with reading or even perhaps with the school. The teacher may have to start by talking about baseball or scouting. Only after a basis of mutual understanding and respect is arrived at can anything be done to teach reading.

G. Occasionally, failure in reading may produce distinct mental disorders.

Some children will be deeply affected by their failure in reading. They may become possessed with a constant anxiety that shows in a lined face and hang-dog manner. They may have hallucinations of being "picked on" or persecuted or followed. They may have fears that show themselves in bad dreams, loss of appetite, twitchings, and other nervous manifestations. Such children should have psychiatric help, and in any event need sympathetic care by all concerned. They need to have their fears set at rest and their self-confidence built up through emphasis on those abilities which they do have. A program of happy play is essential. And equally essential, of course, is the prompt and skillful teaching of reading by a teacher who can be to the child a valued friend.

CHAPTER II

FINDING OUT ABOUT THE CHILD

I. We need to know the child's physical condition.

Teachers and school authorities are still far too prone to believe that we can tell enough about a child's physical condition just by looking at him. Many systems have decided that the teacher is not qualified to inspect children physically and have introduced the school nurse who has had special training. Some schools have gone so far as to require repeated inspection not only by doctors but also by specialists. These schools have in every case been convinced that they should never be without this service. Such experience should be enough to convince all schools that complete knowledge of the physical condition of all children is necessary if the school is to do its duty by them.

Maximum learning by the mind is impossible without maximum efficiency of the body. This is especially true of all conditions which affect mental alertness. It is most obviously the case with conditions of the eyes and ears, which are clearly avenues of learning. We shall now discuss in more detail certain kinds of physical conditions which most strongly affect reading.[1]

A. In what condition are the child's eyes?

The eyes must be used in reading, and for this reason there has been much study and research on eye defects and

---

[1] The teacher should send five cents to the U. S. Government Printing Office for the pamphlet "What Every Teacher Should Know About the Physical Condition of Her Pupils," issued by the U. S. Office of Education.

reading. The summaries of results will be found in various books listed in the bibliography. We shall here take up the things about the eyes that the teacher of reading should watch for. The ideal would be to have every child periodically examined by an eye specialist. In practice, such examining usually follows some observation of defect made by parent or teacher. The teacher therefore has the duty to discover defects whenever possible so that she may urge examination by the eye specialist. She does not take the place of the specialist, but is only trying to get as many handicapped children as possible to go to him.

1. Does the child need correction for vision or astigmatism?

At the first sign of poor reading, a teacher will wonder if the child has proper vision. The child himself will not know, because he believes all people see things as he does. The parents seldom know of eye defects because they do not compare their child with others. The teacher has the best chance to notice whether a child sees as well as other children do. She can watch how he looks at the board. She can see how he holds his book in reading. But no mere observation is satisfactory. Every poor reader should at once have his eyes tested. The commonest method is use of the Snellen Chart with its rows of letters of different sizes. With this chart, eyes are tested one at a time at a distance of twenty feet and with a standard lighting. With a special form of the chart, first graders may be tested. Full directions are given in the pamphlet ''Conserving Children's Eye-Sight'' issued by the National Society for the Prevention of Blindness (New York City). Astigmatism has usually been measured with the wheel chart. The Snellen Chart and wheel chart are useful, but a better method of testing these factors is with the telebinocular, which is described in the next paragraph.

2. Do the child's eyes work together correctly?

Some poor readers have eyes which do not work together properly. For efficient reading, both eyes should easily focus on the same spot at reading distance, which is 13 to 16 inches. The Snellen Chart does not tell whether the eyes fuse properly because with it each eye is tested separately. We have now an instrument, developed from the stereoscope, which measures vision and astigmatism and also tells whether the eyes work together properly both at blackboard distance and at reading distance. The instrument, called the telebinocular,[2] is widely used by teachers who wish to find "suspects," that is, children who need to be sent to the eye specialist for examination. These instruments are now owned by many city school systems or by county superintendents of schools, and every teacher should be able to borrow one to use in examining her pupils. A few minutes for each child is all that is necessary. If there is trouble in eye coördination, eye exercises may help, but these should be prescribed only by the specialist.

---

[2] Information about the telebinocular will be given by the Keystone View Co., Meadville, Pa. Its use is fully discussed in Betts' *The Prevention and Correction of Disability in Reading*. Row Peterson & Co., Evanston, Illinois.

The ophthalmograph, manufactured by the American Optical Co., New York City, will give some of the information that the telebinocular gives. The difference is that the ophthalmograph shows what the eyes do when they are looking at the same object, and the reader may be making them work together in spite of a strong tendency to separate. The strain of overcoming the difficulty may later result in fatigue.

Parents may refuse to take a child to the eye specialist or to get glasses after they are prescribed. Fortunately, many specialists are willing to give free examinations in case of real need, and charitable organizations often supply funds for glasses. If glasses are finally secured, there still remains the problem of getting the child to wear them. Even if efforts in all these directions fail, a knowledge of the child's visual defects enables his teacher to understand his difficulties, and permits her to seat the child properly in the room and to make suitable adjustments in reading matter, seat work and the like.

3. Is the child experiencing eye fatigue?

Some children have developed antagonism to reading because they have found that use of their eyes brings discomfort. Eye strain may cause headaches or even nausea. Often the child may not be clearly conscious of this connection, and it may be very hard for a teacher to detect it. If the telebinocular indicated muscular unbalance, that is, a strong tendency for the eyes to separate or to over-converge, a cause for eye fatigue is suggested. Farsighted eyes are also likely to cause the child discomfort or fatigue. However, if any condition of eye fatigue is noted or suspected, there should be careful examination at once by an eye specialist.

B. What is the state of the child's hearing?

Poor hearing is an important and a long unsuspected cause for poor reading. The child that does not hear well has missed much of what the teacher has said. He has failed to listen to other children's reading because, as we all know, it is very hard to give attention to anything that we do not hear clearly. Poor hearing is often unsuspected because the child is called inattentive and disobedient. Parents are especially unsuspecting of poor hearing because they are so well accustomed to the way their own child acts that they do not realize that he is not acting as a normal child would. The sad thing is that many hearing difficulties are progressive and, if untreated, grow worse year by year.

Poor readers should in every case have their hearing tested. Many schools are now testing all children with the audiometer,[3] an instrument like a phonograph with which as many as forty children can be tested at once. Each child has an ear phone fastened over one ear at a time and listens to numbers, which he writes down. The loudness of the voice giving the numbers slowly decreases, and the point at which the child no longer gets the numbers right tells the degree of hearing deficiency. Retests are advisable of all children making low scores. The audiometer finds "suspects," who should be sent at once to ear specialists.[4] Even if the defect is not corrected, the teacher who has discovered it can make proper allowances in her work. She may seat the child in the best position, stand near him, or otherwise

---

[3] Write to the Western Electric Co., Chicago, for information. Other companies make similar apparatus.

[4] If use of the audiometer cannot be secured, the teacher may use the watch tick test. Place the pupil with his back to the blackboard, and let him close one ear and hold a card beside the opposite eye. Then, place a watch near the open ear and slowly take it further away until he can no longer hear it tick. Mark this spot on the board. Begin further away and bring the watch closer until it is just heard. Mark this spot. Repeat and average the results. Do the same with the other ear. Use a loud ticking "dollar" watch and compare the distances at which the "suspect" can hear with the distance for other children. Definite distances cannot be given because watch ticks differ, but the child with defective hearing will require a much less distance than the average child.

see that he has every chance to know what is going on in class. As soon as he hears easily the reading being done by others, his own reading will have a chance to improve.

Some children who are found by test to have adequate hearing still do not seem to get directions or to know what is going on. Some of these children seem to have difficulty in identifying differences between sounds that are similar. The test for this is to read pairs of words that differ from each other but slightly, and have the child repeat them. The words of one pair may differ only in the initial consonant, or in the final consonant or only in the vowel. A sample test follows. The teacher can make any number of others.

bat	head	coat	most
bad	sled	cut	must
sit	back	red	touch
bit	black	ready	teach
mice	string	study	are
nice	sing	steady	our

If a child does not do this test well, he can be given practice on similar pairs of words. He should be asked to listen closely and to note the small difference in sound, repeating each word exactly as it is said. A short period of such training will usually result in marked improvement, and for this reason the trouble is usually believed to be lack of a habit of attention to sounds. To develop this habit, these children need to be continually watched to see that they repeat completely and accurately all words told them during reading by the teacher. Accurate speaking requires accurate hearing. Some cases are so stubborn, however, as to suggest some innate disability.

C. Has the pupil a speech defect?

A speech defect is a great handicap in the learning of reading. Stuttering or stammering[5] causes a child to refrain from talking and therefore has a general depressing effect on the child's whole language development. A child who seldom talks does not become fluent in use of language. Stuttering also hinders oral reading, thus preventing the teacher from keeping in close touch with the child's progress. If the child is intelligent, however, he will develop silent reading, though more slowly than he might otherwise.

The speech defects that result in mispronunciation cause much greater trouble however. The explanation is that the child who mispronounces words thinks of the words the way he says them and not the way others do. He has, as it were, a language of his own. Now in our ordinary language there is much agreement between the sounds of the letters that make up a word and the sound of the word. There is a natural use of letter-sound cues. In the language of the speech defective child, there is much less agreement. He may say a word or think of the sound of that word in a way that does not agree at all with the letter sounds. Words which sound alike to us may not sound alike to him, and words which to us seem very different may to him seem

---

[5] Every teacher should know that stuttering or stammering is a symptom of a nervous condition and should know how to deal with it. Of the many books on speech defect, *The Jingle Book for Speech Correction,* by Alice Wood (E. P. Dutton & Co., New York, 1934) is perhaps the simplest. The U. S. Office of Education, Washington, D. C., has a pamphlet on Speech Defects that every teacher should have. Send 10c to the Superintendent of Documents for it.

very familiar. Thus part of normal development of reading is blocked. With such a child the first step in remedial reading should be the correction of the speech defect. The mispronunciation may be located by having the child say the alphabet or repeat such a list of words as shown on the speech survey blank in Appendix D. This list presents words that contain the different letters and digraphs and as the child repeats them after the teacher, the exact difficulty is located.

The method of speech correction is essentially to get the child to *hear* the difference between the way he says a word and the way others do. As soon as the child can *hear* the right sound, he is ready to learn by imitation how to *say* the right sound. Children who correct their own defects do so by this process of *hearing* and *imitation*. The pupil may at first want to talk in the old way because it is easier, but the teacher can kindly urge that he pronounce correctly. The change will be gradual. Any phonics in the regular school work, such as word sounding in reading and word analysis in spelling will give opportunity both for ear training and pronouncing. Care must be taken, however, that the child is not made nervous or self-conscious. From a gradual beginning, practice produces progress. Reading will be helped immediately.

D. Is the pupil left-handed?

Much has been written about the relation between handedness and poor reading. Many statistical studies have been made. At first, there seemed to be a markedly greater number of left-handed children among poor readers than normal. Later studies have tended to contradict this impression. The subject is still a matter of study. It is easy to see how left-handedness might contribute to poor reading. In all the years before school, the child watches his hand while he is doing something with it. The left-handed child has naturally been watching his left hand. Now the left hand, in cutting or in drawing or the like, naturally moves from the center of the body toward the left just as the right hand most easily moves from the center of the body to the right. The left-handed child may have therefore acquired the habit of looking at things from right to left or at least looking at the right end first. But in reading we must look from left to right. Therefore it may well be that the left-handed child is more subject than others to confusion in reading habits.

Mirror writing is at times found among poor readers and much significance is sometimes attached to it. It is certainly a sign that the child either perceives differently than others or that in copying what he sees he unconsciously reverses the directions to his muscles. Here again we should not be too much disturbed. We can slowly and carefully build up the correct movements. In extreme cases, it may be advisable to have the child trace over the form of words, letter by letter, from left to right, both to train him in looking at words in that direction and in aiding correct writing. Tracing print is used to help reading; tracing script to help writing if the writing is to be done in script.

Several special methods may sometimes be used with the poor reader who is left-handed. The left-handed reader is likely at first to point to words with his left hand. That hand most naturally moves from right to left. It is therefore advisable to have him follow the line, if at all, with his right hand. It will move naturally from left to right and thus guide the eye in the desired direction. Let him at times count the words he has read, pointing with his right hand. Thus the left-right movement of the eye will be aided also. In some cases it is advisable to have the child lay a blank sheet of paper directly below a line of type and then to copy the line letter-by-letter in print. This compels the movement of both eye and hand from left to right. This has the same effect as the tracing mentioned above.

E. What is the pupil's general health?

Successful reading demands energy, attention, and alertness. Lack of these qualities may sometimes be due to poor health. This condition occurs rather frequently and should be corrected before much progress can be hoped for. If at all possible, full medical examination should be secured. Talks with the mother about the child's eating and other health habits are helpful. Lack of sufficient sleep is often an important cause of inattention and poor work in school. The mother's coöperation must be secured if conditions are to be remedied. Sometimes the giving of special help to the child may be made conditional upon certain improvement of the home situation by the parents. The best device for improving general health conditions for children who need such improvement is the health class that meets once a week after school. A uniformed registered nurse or a medical doctor is the teacher of such a class. Each child who needs help comes with his mother. Health principles are explained to both, and good health practices are recommended. This method has secured surprising results because the nurse or doctor has more authority in this field than the teacher, and because real changes in home conditions usually result.

F. What is the child's past sickness record?

Many children have lost a large part of their primary years of schooling because of sickness. While other children were doing their daily reading lessons, these unfortunate children were home in bed. They missed essential lessons that could not be made up on their return. They failed to learn essential habits. They missed the learning of sight vocabulary. Yet, at the end of the year they were not retained. When absence is due to sickness, there is always a tendency to sympathize with the child and promote him regardless of achievement. Much retardation in reading is due to this situation. When we are seeking to discover reasons for backwardness in reading, we should be sure to inquire concerning past illness and discover how much there was, how serious, and when it occurred.

Another fact to consider is that when a child was seriously ill his mother and family were certain to humor his every whim. For months or for years the mother may have given the child everything he wanted, and required nothing from him. Therefore no attention to any sort of job was developed. As a result, when the child came to school, the teacher's requests or demands were probably ignored. For remedial work with such cases, much kind firmness is required.

Then we must consider the effect of much reading to a sick child by adults. Many children have thus acquired a taste for long and more mature stories that are far beyond primary reading ability. They cannot read what they want to read, and they do not care to read the simple things that they can read. For such cases, skillful choice of materials is very necessary so that by much practice their reading ability may rapidly come to equal their taste.

II. We need to know many aspects of the child's school life.

In the grades, the class room teacher knows a good deal about the individual child after she has had him in her room daily for a number of months. But each year the child goes to a new teacher, and, in most cases, the new teacher must learn all over again the things that the former teacher found out. Cumulative personal records should therefore be kept for all children, but they are especially imperative in remedial reading cases. To build up a record, each teacher may write out a statement about each child leaving her care, the statements to be kept in folders for other teachers and for administrative officers, and to be seen by no one else. It is especially important that no parent ever be allowed to see these records. They are frank statements for the eye of the impartial, scientifically minded person alone, and no parent can ever be such a person as far as his own child is concerned. If a cumulative record is not to be thus kept confidential, it has to be restricted to objective data, such as tests, measurements, examinations and the like.

If a teacher is to make a statement for the guidance of other teachers, she should try to cover those points that future teachers will want to know about. She should relate events and tell facts that will tell the future teacher what to look out for and anticipate. We shall point out what some of these facts may be. If no records such as these exist, the teacher in charge of a remedial case should go to former teachers and ask for confidential information on important points. Parents may also have to be interviewed. If a doctor has examined the child, he will also be able to give valuable information.

A. Does the pupil like school?

Success in remedial reading requires the pupil's coöper-ation. Therefore the first question is, "What is his attitude towards school and things connected with school?" The reading teacher may have asked others this question but she will be cautious in accepting the answer since it is very easy to be mistaken about a child's attitudes. She will especially seek to find out the pupil's attitude as she talks with him to secure his confidence. If she finds out that the child likes school, she knows that the child will be eager to learn to read so that he may succeed in school work. If he does not like school, she will have to make an approach through something that he does like. The child's success will be in direct proportion to his effort. Effort must be secured through some existing interest. Some of these interests are discussed below.

B. What school subjects does he like?

Even if a child is a failure in reading, he may be good at arithmetic. A child who is proud of his skill with numbers will realize that he has to read the problems in the arithmetic book. Or the child may be good at drawing or some other school subject. He may even like to hear geography or history stories when read by others. Some children actually like a subject of which they as yet have been unable to read a word. The teacher can get the pupil to talk about the things he likes or does well and thus make closer contact with him. She may be able to find easy reading materials that deal with favorite school subjects and thus secure greater motive in reading. The remedial teacher needs to be well acquainted with many easy reading books (see Appendix C) and magazines so that she can provide something that will appeal to the special interests of deficient readers. The great problem is to find something that the child *wants* to read, and a special interest in some school subject may furnish the answer. The school may have given achievement tests in the school subjects but these records may not give a picture of the child's special abilities because a reading handicap will prevent him from making the showing he should. The achievement and interest in school subjects can be easily discovered, however, through informal conversation.

C. Does the child play freely and as an equal with the children of his grade?

Inquiries about playground and extra-curricular activities reveal a great deal about the child's personality development. Play is a large part of any child's life. In fact, a child is likely to be more himself at play than at any other time. Knowledge about the child's play activities is absolutely necessary in problem cases of remedial reading, both for the correction of personality difficulties and for discovery of interests.

The way a child plays with others tells a great deal about his social development. If he is accepted by others of his age, failure in reading apparently has not produced social maladjustment as yet. If the child does not play normally with others, a sense of inferiority probably exists. The child may show this by standing apart and wistfully looking on. Or he may show it by pushing himself forward in an unnatural and obstreperous way. Poor reading may be a partial cause of the situation. Failure in class may have set the child apart from the others. The promise that he can learn to read "like everybody else" may have a splendid effect. Or the situation may be reversed; social maladjustment may be a cause of poor reading. A child may be set apart because of some undesirable trait and may therefore lose all interest in keeping up with the others in school work. Thus reading failure and social maladjustment may interact, each intensifying the other.

Whether or not the child plays with children of his own age and grade is important. A very strong sign of mental immaturity is playing with children who are younger. When we do not have intelligence tests, we must estimate mental maturity somehow. Watching the child on the playground is an excellent method. In that way we can compare his behavior with that of other children of the same age or of children who are younger or older. If a ten-year-old child acts like a nine-year-old, we may suspect that he has only nine-year-old development. Teachers who have observed many children at play can watch a single individual for a time and give an excellent estimate of the stage of mental development. The best single indication is the age of the children the child habitually plays with. Of course, home and neighborhood conditions should be known before a final opinion is reached.

D. Is the pupil good at playground activities or other extra-curricular work?

The teacher wishes to find some interest which she can build upon in the remedial work. Sometimes school subjects will not furnish this basis, but school activities will. The teacher will therefore inquire what games he has a special interest in, whether he likes to sing or draw or take part in class room plays, and so on. By this means she may find some interest which she can use as a beginning for remedial work. It is a rare child indeed who is not good at something, and that something will furnish a basis for a program that will spread ultimately to a full, rounded life.

E. How many non-promotions has the child had and when and why?

We cannot very well form a judgment about a child's reading situation unless we know something of his past school record. This does not mean his past grades in reading, for those grades are influenced by many things besides reading achievement. What we do want to know is how many years the child has been in school and whether the conditions in those years were favorable or unfavorable. The first question, naturally, is whether the child is the usual age for his grade. If he is older, was the reason sickness, changing from one school to another, or non-promotion? Changing from school to school has the same disturbing effect as sickness, taking a child out of the routine so that he loses step and loses interest. In these days when parents move about more than formerly, much poor reading by children results.

If there was non-promotion in the child's experience, in what year of school life did it come? Non-promotion at any time is a tremendous discouragement to any child, but its effect upon reading varies with the level of development. The later non-promotion occurred, the more significant it is. Failure the first year may indicate merely a slow start. Failure after three years in school probably indicates three years of failure to learn.

Reasons for non-promotion can sometimes be found from cumulative records, mentioned on page 19, if such records have been kept. Another method is conversations with the child's previous teachers, if those teachers are still in the system. Conversations with such teachers are enlightening in two ways. Those teachers can tell a great deal about a child's behavior and his reaction to reading and other activities. At the same time those teachers will be revealing the sort of treatment which they gave the child and the methods they attempted to use. We could understand most of a child's difficulties if we could only know the way he has been handled by the school in past years.

III. We need to know some aspects of the child's home life.

When the child is at school, we see only part of his life. The other part goes on in the home or in situations produced by the home. Now the part of the child's life that we see at school is more an outgrowth of home life than is usually recognized. Many schools, knowing this fact, have visiting teachers who find out the home background of school problem cases. Other schools expect teachers to visit the homes of all their children. And all good teachers have always made it a point to become acquainted with the homes of those children who are having reading difficulty. Reading failure is so often connected with home conditions that we may definitely say we must know some things about the home situation of every remedial case.

A. Does the child coöperate happily with his parents?

A child's general state of happiness has a great deal to do with his success or failure at school. The child who is unhappy at home is greatly handicapped. Therefore we must try to learn whether the child and parents get along together. Sometimes it is important to learn whether the child is closer to mother or father and what interest each parent takes in the child's school work. A very unfavorable effect on a child's school work is also produced when there is quarreling between parents or when the presence of relatives or of strangers in the home makes it an unhappy place.

Unhappy home conditions disturb a child's sleep and rest, and tend to make him nervous and tired. They often have a suppressing effect that slows up or stops activity in school and makes the child inclined to just "sit" instead of learn. Home conditions may also make a child rebellious and antagonistic to all authority. Or there may just be an emotional disturbance that shows itself in moodiness and brooding. Only the happy child can learn at his best. If a child is unhappy, we need to see whether the home does not explain the situation.

B. What are the ages, grade placement, and school success of his brothers and sisters?

A child's school attitudes and school success are greatly influenced by the work of brothers and sisters. A frequent situation is for the poor reader to have an older brother or sister who did well in school and who learned to read easily. The parents, in a mistaken attempt to motivate the child, are then constantly holding up this brother or sister as an example. If the child admires that brother or sister, some urging is beneficial, but too much urging produces quite the opposite result. A child who constantly hears about the reading of a smart brother or sister is very likely to become permanently resentful over the whole business and to make no further effort to learn. Yet parents seldom realize the damage they are doing and often have to be told to cease making any comparisons between the one child and the other.

A still worse situation, however, is for a smart younger brother or sister to catch up with the poor reader in school. Here not only parents but classmates make constant slighting remarks to the older child. It is small wonder that such a child becomes a conduct problem as well as gives up all attempt to learn to read. Whenever such unfortunate relations exist, there must be some talk with parents to explain the damage being done and to secure sympathetic coöperation. At the same time every effort must be made to get success in reading so that the child's self-respect may be restored.

C. What home hobbies does the child have?

Home hobbies may form an excellent basis for remedial reading. The boy who builds airplanes will be glad to attack stories about airplanes or to try to read directions for making them. Every collection that a child may have made is a possible basis for an interest in reading. Every pet may furnish a basis for interest. Talking about home hobbies gives an excellent chance for friendly understanding between child and the remedial reading teacher.

As noted above the teacher needs to know where to locate easy stories related to hobbies. Many will be found in the new primary readers that are not marked for grades.

D. What does the child want to be when he grows up?

Some children have very definite ideas as to the future work they want to do. Some want to be mechanics, some want to be aviators, some farmers, and so on. Such plans furnish an important basis for remedial reading. First, they enable a teacher to emphasize how reading is needed in the kind of position the child is thinking of. Sometimes, as in the case of town children who want to be farmers, the child may believe that no reading will be needed. His belief will be shaken if the teacher shows him a number of bulletins of the U. S. Department of Agriculture. These bulletins will have interesting pictures and the child will realize he can not tell much about the pictures unless he can read what is under them. He must also realize that the farmer reads the newspapers as well as do all other intelligent people. Similarly, children who expect to be shop or factory workers in cities imagine that they will not need much reading. Such children need to be shown that all workers need to read directions, instructions, and the like, and that workers who wish to advance must study their special jobs through books and special magazines.

Second, the teacher will find it possible to use reading materials connected with the desired occupation. For instance, one boy who had refused to learn to read was started by being taught the names of the different makes of cars just because he planned some day to work on automobiles. Naturally, the use of future occupations is possible only with some children, since many of them have no future plans.

E. Does the child work after school hours, and at what?

Many boys have part-time work after school hours. The same use may be made of such work as of future occupations. First, some reading may be needed in the part-time work, and second, use may be made of the interest the work gives. A boy who sells magazines may be approached through some titles showing the contents of the magazines.

The boy who works in a grocery store can learn to read labels.

The teacher may tell a good deal about the child's personality and get a chance for closer contact through knowing the kind of work the boy does and what he does with the money he earns.

CHAPTER III

HOW WELL DOES HE READ?

I. We need to know certain facts about the child's reading.[1]

When we are told that a child is a poor reader, we need to find out just how poor he is and what special handicaps or weaknesses he may have. Reading tests will be given to determine these facts, but the teacher will not want to give these tests immediately. Since to do so might discourage the child still further and hinder the making of friendly contact. Instead she will want to learn informally what is the state of the child's reading. It is this informal approach that we shall discuss here.

A. What is the grade level of the books the child reads easily?

Remedial reading must start from where the child is. It must start with something the child can do with relative ease and therefore with pleasure. It must start back with the child's present reading ability no matter how far back that may be. There must be no doubt about this. It is much better to go farther back than necessary than not to go back far enough. Therefore our first question is, "What kind of a reading selection can the pupil go through smoothly and with pleasure, thinking of the story rather than of the words?"

To answer this question the teacher should try the pupil out on a modern series of readers in which the books have

---

[1] A form for the regular teacher to fill out to aid the remedial teacher is found in Appendix A. Its sections are explained in the last chapter and the present one.

no grade markings.[2] She can have a set of these and have the child read something from several of the volumes. She should first give him a book that will certainly be easy for him and follow it by the next harder, and so on. If the first book she gives him is too hard, she can hand him the next easier. She can thus rapidly get an answer to the question, "What is the grade level of the books the child reads easily?" The caution here is to be sure to *start* with an easy enough book. In most cases it is safest to begin with a primer if a story can be selected that is not about very young children.

B. Does the child know common words easily by sight?

No one can read without an adequate sight vocabulary. The common words must be recognized instantly so that the attention can be directed to the few new words and to what the sentences say. Poor readers invariably have an insufficient sight vocabulary. They failed to get the usual sight word knowledge in the early years when other children were getting it. They may have been absent, or inattentive, or immature, but, whatever the cause, the efforts of primary teachers and primary books to teach the common words failed to take effect. A teacher can note this defect by listening to a child read any simple material. The more simple the material, the larger the proportion of frequently used words, and it will be instantly apparent if a child hesitates over the simple words, such as, *had, for, little*, which have been met with continually in reading matter and should be instantly known to the child by sight.

---

[2] The Children's Bookshelf, Ginn & Co., Boston, is a very useful series of this type.

One would think that a child at any grade level, who has struggled somehow through a good many school books, would be certain to have learned the everyday words by sight. This probably fails to happen because repetitions of these words do not come close enough together. Books beyond the primary grades have an ever increasing burden of new words which so confuse the child that he is not conscious that he has met some of the words before. Primary books plan to teach sight words; later books do not. Consequently, if poor readers are to develop a sight vocabulary, we must take them back to primary books or use some special method such as is described in the next section.

C. How many words of the basic sight vocabulary does he know instantly?

A teacher can quickly discover what sight vocabulary a child has by using the Basic Sight Vocabulary Cards. This set of cards presents in primer type 220 common words which make up more than 50 per cent of all reading matter. In fact, they make up 60 per cent or more of most school books. The list of words appear in Appendix A. These words form the framework, so to speak, of all reading matter because they include prepositions, conjunctions, pronouns, adjectives, adverbs and the most common verbs. Nouns are not included because nouns necessarily change as subject matter changes. The words are on cards of convenient size which are placed before the child at reading distance and then turned as rapidly as possible. The most rapid turning will be at the rate of not more than a hundred and twenty words per minute, and these words should be recognized at least at that rate if reading is to be satisfactory at all.

Readers of average third grade ability are generally found to know all, or practically all, of the 220 words. Children of a lower grade level can be expected to know only the most common ones on the list. If the child's grade placement indicates that these words should be known and they are found not to be known, they can be taught by intensive work in a very short time. They are treated as a game and the child keeps his own improvement curve until he "wins," that is, until he knows them all.[3]

Caution needs here to be given that a very bashful fearful child should not at the very first be run through a test on these 220 words if he is likely to fail on most of them. No child should be discouraged at the very start. But if the test is given just as a game, without embarrassment to a child, it is a very great help in diagnosing reading difficulties. See Appendix C for full direction for the use of these cards.

D. Does the pupil miscall words and read right on, or does he correct his mistakes?

In ordinary reading, one gives words a mere hasty glance, and there is always the likelihood that he may mistake one word for another. The usual check against mistakes of this kind is that the resulting sentences do not make sense. It is important, in listening to a poor reader, to notice whether he uses this check upon his recognition of words. He is very likely to call many of them incorrectly, but does he discover that he has done so? If the child reads nonsense and goes right on, it indicates he needs to learn to pay attention to the sense of what he reads. If he

---

[3] These cards may be secured from the Garrard Press, Champaign, Ill.

realizes he has miscalled words, it is a much more hopeful sign, and the child may be able by self-correction to help build up his own sight vocabulary.

E. Does the pupil try to sound out new words, and if so, what success does he have?

Some children do nothing with words which they do not recognize by sight, but simply look up at the teacher. Other children will attempt in some way or other to sound out strange words. A teacher can sometimes tell the method used by listening to the child's whispering to himself. Sometimes she can ask the child to sound out a word which she thinks may be possible for him. Mispronunciations will tell something of the way the child sounds letters or word parts. For future use, a record of mispronunciations can be made without the child's knowledge as is done in the Gray Oral reading paragraphs. That is, a word can be spelled as the child pronounced it, using proper marking to show the sound. Usually, when the poor reader tries to pronounce, certain definite difficulties will appear. (1) He may be entirely unable to pronounce certain letters or digraphs. (2) He may get all the letters right, but be unable to blend them into a word. (3) He may sound the separate letters in digraphs. (4) He may pronounce all vowels long or all vowels short. (5) Or there may be certain definite mispronunciations of letters or syllables. This study of what the child does with sounding will tell what remedial teaching of sounding is required. Further discussion of sounding is to be found on pages 82 to 87.

F. How well does the pupil comprehend easy material?

If a child cannot read anything at all, we need not consider comprehension. But if we can give him, in the way suggested above, some material which he can actually read, we should note carefully what his comprehension is. The expression with which he reads is some indication of understanding. A better one is the ability to tell the gist of what he is reading. We can ask him to repeat the story. We can ask him to answer simple questions which ordinary comprehension should make possible. We are here dealing, of course, with ordinary reading and should expect no more understanding than ordinary reading should give. At higher school levels, where study is stressed, special testing is necessary to tell how well a child can study.

G. What are the pupil's eye movement habits?

If the school system has an instrument for photographing eye movements,[4] it is of interest to get a record of the pupil's eye movements by its use. If the child can actually read easy material, he has developed certain eye movement habits, which are shown on the film. However, such a child's chief trouble is with reading matter that has words that are of unknown meaning or are hard to pronounce. What a child does with such difficulties is best understood through hearing oral reading. In fact, to the remedial reading teacher, the photographing of eye movements is chiefly a verification of information that she has already obtained by other methods. In reading clinics, such verification is necessary, and eye photograph data are used for scientific studies. Full discussion of the ophthalmograph and the metronoscope are to be found in Appendix E.

---

[4] Literature describing this machine, the ophthalmograph, may be secured from the American Optical Company, New York City.

H. Does the pupil show lip movements?

If a poor reader moves his lips, we know he is making the sound of each word he reads. This fact may indicate various things. First, he may be still in the primary stage in which the word form has no meaning for him unless he thinks its sound. All readers begin at this stage. Many poor readers are still in it but do not reveal the fact by any lip movements. Second, the reader may be using his lips only because he is trying to sound out words that he does not recognize. A child often has a poor sight vocabulary and must therefore attempt to sound out many words that should instead be recognized instantly. Third, the pupil may be perfectly capable of reading without lip movement if he hurried up his reading a bit so that lip movement would be inconvenient. His sounding may not be necessary at all but just the accompaniment of slow reading.

Each of these cases requires different treatment. It is no use asking the first case, the very poor reader, to read without sounding because he cannot do so. The second case, the child who is sounding out strange words, will naturally use his lips. He cannot stop doing so until he recognizes the words directly, that is, by looks and not by sound. The third case, the child who could read without lip movement if he read faster, needs to be speeded up, chiefly by practice on easy material. When his thinking as he reads goes faster than his speaking speed, he will stop moving his lips just as all the rest of us stopped the practice somewhere in our reading experience. When we could read faster than we could speak, we stopped pronouncing because we had to.

There are occasional cases in which lip reading cannot be avoided. Some few individuals seem to be auditory minded to the extent that they can never get meaning from print except through sounding. Such persons' speed of reading will never exceed their speed of speaking. They have a permanent handicap, which means that reading will always take them more time than it does others.

In Chapters II and III we have discussed the various items listed in the Reading Case Report that appears in Appendix A. These items give a good general picture of the child who is having reading difficulty. As our discussions have made clear, however, each item admits of great extension. Study of the child's physical condition can be carried much further by specialists and should in some cases be carried into much more detail. Aspects of the child's home life can be much further studied by a social worker or a visiting teacher. Aspects of the school life can be studied much further by an interested teacher, and most teachers will, in fact, know these aspects much more fully than we have suggested. The facts concerning the child's reading need more study and they shall be our special concern in the rest of this book. We have so far dealt with reading only in its most general aspects. We shall now have to approach the remedial reading problems that arise in the various levels of the school.

CHAPTER IV

REMEDIAL READING FOR PRIMARY GRADES

Since we wish to consider remedial problems as they present themselves to teachers in the school, we shall deal with these problems under the larger grade division of primary, middle grades, upper grades and high school. This is not the approach of the clinic but it is of necessity the approach of the teacher. She has a certain post in the school system and she must work at that post. She wishes to know the troubles that are likely to come to her and what to do with them. Hence our treatment by grade divisions.

I. A chief cause of remedial reading in primary grades is beginning children in the school on the basis of chronological age alone.

Children naturally differ in the rate with which they mature. Therefore if all children entered first grade at exactly six years of chronological age, there would still be a considerable spread in maturity or mental development. The spread in development of a typical class of beginners, all of exactly six years chronological age, would (according to the recent researches of Terman) be roughly as follows:

2 7½ years mental age
4 7 years mental age
6 6½ years mental age
8 6 years mental age
6 5½ years mental age
4 5 years mental age
2 4½ years mental age
──
32

Of course this exact theoretical distribution seldom if ever occurs, but it does suggest the differences in ability that may be in a group of beginners. When we consider that most schools admit some children at even less than 6 years chronological age, it is evident that a great spread of ability is nearly always to be expected.

In a situation such as this, some children may be ready to begin reading shortly after entering school, some may not be ready until after Christmas, and some may not be ready until the very end of the year. This spread in readiness to read is the natural result of entering children on chronological age. On top of this practice, the schools move most of the children on at the end of the first year. Of those entering grade two, therefore, some may be ready for second readers, some may be ready for first readers, and some may be ready only for primers. The fast learners get further and further ahead, and the slow learners get further and further behind. So in the second grade we usually have children who are already a year behind the supposed norm, and in third grade we have children who are already more than a year behind. This remedial reading situation is almost universal in the primary grades and arises naturally from the usual school practices. How can this situation be met?

A. A common solution to this problem is retention in grade I.

Many schools retain a fifth or more of first graders at the end of the year. These are the children who if passed into grade two would be a year behind. That is, in grade two they would still be only beginning readers. By retaining them, we make them perhaps normal beginners for grade one. Then in grade two there will be no children who are more than six months behind the average. If the children passed on into grade two spread out in achievement as is usual, the slow ones falling more and more behind, the very slowest might be retained there. Consequently the lowest group going into grade three will at least be ready for books of grade two, and thus not more than a year behind. In this way we may avoid having such retarded groups in grades two and three.

Strongly in favor of this practice is the fact that if, as a result of slow mental development rate, some children are certain to be retained at some time during the grades, the best place to retain them is in grade one. At this point there is the least suffering from disappointment and from failure to go on with friends. Then the child who has been retained in grade one has, from that time on, throughout his school life, the advantage of being one year older than his companions. Thus his mental development may equal theirs and he will have had one extra year of experience. This fact may compensate a great deal for slower mentality or slower maturity.

Against this practice of retention is the argument that children should never fail and that the groups should go on as a unit. Advocates of this view believe that we should keep children of the same chronological age together for social adjustment reasons. They admit that great variation in reading ability will result in each grade, but they would rather meet that variation than use the method of retaining pupils. In actual practice we have a combination of these two views. Poor readers are retained under some circumstances and promoted under other circumstances.

The tendency is toward more general promotion, and this means more provision for poor readers in all grades.

B. A practical solution is retention in the kindergarten until reading readiness is attained.

Many schools are now retaining children in the kindergarten until they are ready to attack reading successfully. The assumption is that all children will then start beginning reading with about an equal chance of success, and that in the primary grades at least, there will be little need for remedial reading. This method is justifiable to parents on the ground that the school is giving the child the training he needs instead of the first grade work that will make him unhappy because he cannot do it. The kindergarten can be used to develop socialization, coördination and attention and then can develop special aspects of reading readiness. Therefore where the school has a kindergarten, retention of slow learners there is usually the best policy, together with special measures for securing reading readiness.

C. A pre-reading class in grade I is a common plan that serves the purpose very well.

A pre-reading class in grade I is really a sort of temporary kindergarten. It trains the child in the needed school habits. It develops attention and coördination. It has the great advantage of being under the direction of the reading teacher. She will know the type of activities and work books to use. She will use books for coloring and cutting to train the eyes to fixate steadily as needed in reading. Such activities also train the child to give his attention steadily to a job as is needed in a reading lesson. The teacher will use labels and will print directions on the board, thus teaching the idea that words are meaningful. She will use materials that develop left to right eye movement. In fact, she will doubtless use several of the pre-reading picture books or reading readiness work books that are now on the market. At the same time, since the pre-reading class are in the same room with those who are reading, they are stimulated to a desire to learn to read. The pre-reading class in the First Grade room is the natural solution when all children must enter first grade on chronological age alone.

The pre-reading class saves the children from the initial failure that is bound to follow attempting to read too soon and thus ensures that they begin reading with enthusiasm and with success. It cannot, however, push the slow children so that they catch up with the fast ones. By this system, the fast children begin reading in September, some children perhaps in January, and some perhaps not until April or May. At the end of the year the system is presented with the two alternatives already discussed. One is the retention of the slow children, with some disappointment of children and parents, but perhaps not a major hurt to personality because these children will be the leaders in grade I next year and will be able to hold their own for years because they are one year older than their companions. The other alternative is passing these children on, with the provision that the second grade teacher begin teaching them where they really are. That is, the slowest ones will begin primers in grade II. Some of these retarded for reasons other than mentality may develop rapidly and catch up with the others, but most will steadily slide further behind because of slow development. It will be necessary to retain them either in the second or third grade if they are to be sufficiently advanced to do real reading as they begin grade four. If this retention is not made, and the children are pushed ahead year after year, there will be serious remedial cases in grade four, at which point it will become almost impossible to adapt the work to the very poor readers.

D. The primary school is the most recent suggestion.

Some schools have attempted to solve both the reading problem and the promotion problem by institution of a primary school. They do not have kindergarten or primary grades but enroll the children in the primary school in which they are to stay until able to do fourth grade reading. In the primary school there are not three grades but a large number of groups at different levels of development. Each group is as homogeneous as possible and children can be shifted at any time from one to another. Each group progresses at its own best rate. It is expected that most children will spend three years in the primary school but some may spend two and some may spend four or more. A child does not come to the end of the primary school and fail. He gradually shifts from group to group year after year so that he progresses continually but slowly. When he finally comes to the end of the primary school, he is ready for fourth grade reading and so goes on. This plan is proving highly successful wherever conditions make it possible. It attains the ideal of each child in a group that suits his own abilities; it removes the need for singling out individuals for remedial work in the primary grades; and it practically eliminates remedial reading from grade

IV. The requirements for success are a large enough number of groups to fit a good many stages of development, and teachers who can make their work very flexible.

II. **Proper treatment of slow or remedial groups in primary grades requires that both teachers and parents be convinced that children must work at the level at which they really are.**

Strangely enough, many teachers and parents have the set idea that first graders must be given a first reader, second graders must be given a second reader, and third graders must be given a third reader. They have the idea that giving the child the proper graded book will make him a reader of that grade level. Perhaps this idea comes from the fact that we do learn fourth grade arithmetic from a fourth grade book, and fifth grade spelling from a fifth grade book, and so on. But reading is not knowledge. It is a slowly developed skill. If a child cannot lift a twenty pound weight, we do not teach him by giving him a twenty pound weight. We give him a ten pound weight instead and gradually work up to the twenty pounds. Thus, one does not learn second grade reading out of a second reader. One learns to read second readers only by being able to read first readers. A child learns to read third readers only by reading second readers. The child works up step by step. We must find the step the child is now on, master that step, then master the next, and so on. We cannot schedule the learning of reading as we schedule a train. No teacher can be sure just how well a group will be able to read by a certain time. She will keep them going but they may go fast or slow. She cannot force or push them. But parents do not know this. They want the teacher to "make" the child learn to read. They try to force the child to do so. They think of reading as "learning" which to them means something like memorizing. Instead, reading is growing, just as much as growing in height and weight. And the child must grow from where he is. He cannot do otherwise.

A. If necessary, the child can be in a "regular reading class," with the remedial work as "review reading."

If it is necessary to do so to placate parents, the child can be allowed to sit as usual in his regular reading class, even though he does no more than look at the book and listen to the others read. Then in another class, or at another time by himself, he can be given training in "review reading." Everyone has the idea that review is a good thing in all subjects. Why not in reading? It is in this class that the child would be really learning. Sometimes, sitting in the regular class may have a harmful influence, giving the child a sense of failure or of resentment. Sometimes the child may benefit from the regular class through listening to the others, or through his attempts to recognize some of the words in his book. Each child must be considered as an individual case, and the best arrangement made for him.

B. The ideal is for parent and school to recognize that each child will work best only at his real working level.

It is splendid if a whole school system can get on to the basis of recognizing differences in skill and frankly having the children work "where they are." This gets away from much pretense and artificial arrangement. This change to a basis of real skill can best be made by use of standard tests. These have nation-wide norms and have authority with all persons concerned. Of course, nation-wide norms must be used with caution, as they often do not fit the local situation. Local norms can be used instead, that is, averages for grades or rooms that show what most of the children are doing and therefore which children are doing better or worse. But if the idea of standard performances in skills is recognized, there will be much more frankness with parents, and much more drive on the part of the children. If children can be brought to face their own weaknesses, as proved by tests, and not to excuse or to gloss them over, they will do their best to improve. The only unfortunate situation is with children of low intelligence who are by nature handicapped in achieving the same levels of skills as the average. These children demand special treatment in ways that are too complicated to discuss here. But even for them, the recognition of real standards by all persons, including parents, is healthful if managed rightly.

This means that children in any grade will be given the books that they can read with pleasure and profit. It means, therefore, that the second grade will start with some groups using second readers, some first readers, and some primers. The third grade will have groups using third readers, second readers and first readers, with a few children receiving special work with primers. Every class in every school may not conform to this pattern but the principle will be applied "Each child reading a book he *can* read."

III. Remedial groups or cases in primary grades can use usual materials and methods.

A. New books at the lower reading level should be secured.

Poor readers in primary grades, unless much older than others because of retardation, can be put back to the place where they really belong in reading. If very poor, they can be given pre-primers, no matter what grade they are in. After becoming able to read easily at that level, they can be given primers, and thus work up from level to level. There must be no hurrying to higher levels. Slow learners must read more books at each level than better learners. It is important to be sure these are *new* reading books. In old ones the stories are already known and there can be little interest and little real reading. Also, if new books are purchased for the slow readers, they will be proud of them and be envied by the other children. Flash cards and word drills can also be used just as they are used in first grade. This going back can be made something of a game, and thus the process made more attractive. There may be a little objection to using the "baby" materials but usually not too much. Usually the work is so much easier than the regular work that real pleasure is found in it, and the reading is fun for the first time. Of course, some judgment can be used so as to choose pre-primers and primers that do not too much suggest very small children, and that are about pets or airplanes, or other things that all children are interested in.

B. The slow group in a room can be handled by various methods.

Usually the remedial cases make up a third or a fourth group in the second or third grade. If the teacher is too busy, she can often turn this group over part of the time to one of the more mature pupils who has the natural abilities that will make her a good manager of other children. The work of the helper will be largely having the children read little stories and telling them the words they do not know. In these beginning books, words are repeated so often that repeated telling will cause learning. Or the pupil-teacher can conduct word games or word drills. A good one is for the leader to show a word card and have the children find the word on the page before them or see how often they can find it on the page. This gives practice at word comparison and critical looking at words. A plan successfully used even in second grade is to have a library or book period for the whole room and to seat the good readers and poor readers in alternate rows. All children will be reading different books, suited to their different abilities and interest selected from the reading table or room library. The poor readers will be instructed, if they get stuck on a word to point to it and show it to the child in the next row. He will be able to pronounce the word with little interruption of his own reading. This pronouncing will be the only speaking done. The teacher can move about and see that all are at work, especially helping the poor readers in selection of books or in recognizing hard words. Thus the poor readers get quantity of practice, which is just what they need.

C. **Sounding attack and use of context must be emphasized, but immediate recognition should have first place.**

Poor readers in primary grades also need help with a sounding attack. When they stop at a word, they should always be asked, ''How does the word begin?'', thus emphasizing beginning consonants. If this beginning sound is rightly given, the question may be, "Then what do you think the word is? What word that begins that way would fit into the story?" This emphasizes guessing from context. If there is enough maturity, words can be sounded through entire and help given in blending sounds into words. But sounding attack should not be emphasized until the common words are known instantly by sight. Words should be recognized instantly if possible. Sounding should not be allowed to become a habitual method for words which should be instantly recognized. To prevent this, it is often advisable for the teacher to give the word immediately as soon as the child hesitates, and then to ask him to point to the word and say it, thus practicing the association of the whole word with sound of the whole word.

It should be noted that the regular phonics program of the primary grades needs to be adjusted to remedial cases. We have pointed out that sight recognition of the common words must come first. Then the phonics work must be introduced very gradually. Pushing phonics too fast has been the chief cause of failure of children to learn use of sounding. There is such a thing as phonics readiness, meaning that a certain mental maturity, probably seven years of mental age, is necessary before we can expect use of the principles of sounding.[1]

---

[1] See Phonics Readiness, E. W. Dolch. *Elementary School Journal,* Nov., 1937. Also Phonics and Polysyllables, E. W. Dolch. *Elementary English Review,* April, 1938.

IV. In primary grades, we should think of and plan for slow progress groups rather than for "remedial" work.

In the first years of school, the chief concern is adjustment to other children, to school, and to activity learning. Reading is a tool that is acquired during the process but it is far from the all important center of interest it is sometimes made. Our chief concern with reading is that by the end of the third year there be a genuine interest in reading matter as something full of meaning and usefulness, and enough skill to permit profitable attack on the texts and library facilities that will be met with in grade IV. In the primary division, therefore, we watch chiefly for well rounded healthy development, but keep a sharp eye upon the reading adjustment. If that adjustment is not coming along, we make sure the child has attractive materials at his real working level and keep calling attention to sight vocabulary, simple sounding, and use of context.

CHAPTER V

INDIVIDUAL REMEDIAL READING

I. Every teacher should have the experience of doing individual remedial reading.

There is no way of learning about reading that is quite as effective as doing individual remedial reading. Even teachers who are teaching primary reading in the class room never get quite the insight that they would through work with an individual. Teachers who are going to do group remedial work should, above all, have the experience of doing individual work first. The reason is that, in dealing with a group, it is very difficult to discover what the different individuals are doing or how they are doing it. The class carries out a certain exercise and then goes on. With the individual, the case is very different. It is not a question of doing certain things and going on. Instead, it is a question of getting certain results, and there is no going on until those results are secured. One tries one method and another method and keeps on trying until there is success. The teacher is compelled to find out what the child's mental processes are. Teachers of long experience have repeatedly testified that the most enlightening experience they have ever had was in struggling with a remedial reading case. All training of teachers of reading should provide for such experience. It would also be an excellent thing if every year each teacher in service should definitely take charge of an individual case and stick with it until results were secured. This one case would give the teacher an understanding of teaching problems that would be of great benefit to all her students.

A. Ideally, remedial reading should always be individual.

The process of reading is made up of many skills, habits, and attitudes. In each one of these there may be a natural disability, or bad habits, or inadequate learning. The number of possible combinations of these various defects is almost infinite and each child has a new and different combination. Therefore, each child really presents a new and different problem. Reading clinics, which know cases most thoroughly, find always that no two are alike. It is only when we treat cases somewhat superficially that we can think of them as being alike. It is therefore no exaggeration to say that for the best results each child should be handled in a distinctive way that is suited to his particular case and not as well suited to any other. Ideally, therefore, all remedial work should be individual.

B. Personality problems must be handled individually.

Failure in reading produces personality difficulties, as we have explained in Chapter I. Obviously these cannot be handled very well by group methods. Only by individual study of each case and individual treatment of each case can much help be given. It is not enough to say that we will correct the reading defect and other things will correct themselves. Wrong attitudes and complexes are not completely removed merely by enabling the child to read, and often the child will not learn to read unless the personality problems are handled first. Dealing with personality difficulties is and always will be an individual matter.

C. Group remedial reading merely tries to do the same thing as individual reading but under different conditions.

As we have said, ideally all remedial reading should be individual. If every teacher would take an individual case every year, as we have suggested, there could be a great deal of individual work and the number of poor readers would be rapidly diminished. Perhaps some day our methods and materials may be such that there will be no failures in reading. Meanwhile there are and will continue to be many cases of trouble with reading, and some plan for handling them is necessary. That plan is group remedial reading. Methods used in such work will be discussed in detail later but it will there be noted that all group methods are an attempt to do under the handicap of numbers what can be done better individually. That is why teachers who intend to do group work should have the experience of doing individual work first.

II. The non-reader is the most difficult problem.

The essence of remedial work is to go back to where the child really is and go on from there. In reading, this means to start with something the child can actually read. But with the non-reader there is nothing he can actually read. We cannot start with any reading at all. The non-reader is one who just does not know enough words of any kind to read the simplest sentences.

Non-readers appear in all the grades. In grade II we would not call the child a non-reader but a delayed reader. He can be taught to read by the regular methods used in all beginning reading. With the immature child of second or third grade, the use of very simple but very interesting stories is still possible. Very attractive pictures are important. There are some pre-primers which can be used because they do not deal merely with the playing of very small children. Some of these deal with animals. Some deal with special festival days. They have the pictures, they have the story appeal, and they have the very simple vocabulary that is necessary. In re-teaching reading at this level, there is almost a repetition of the usual beginning book work except that stories which would be thought "baby stories" are avoided.

In grade IV, however, or even in grade III if the child is nine years old or more, the child who cannot read at all cannot be treated as a mere beginner. We call him a non-reader and must deal with him in ways suited to his age and condition.

A. We must at once attack the non-reader's sense of failure.

A child who has been in school more than two years and has not learned to read knows that he has failed. He has been told about it by every one. As a result he may have given up, become antagonistic, or developed any other of the reactions discussed in Chapter I. Therefore, the teacher who tries to help the non-reader must direct all her efforts towards getting success from the start. Even the very first meeting must leave the child with a sense of accomplishment and therefore of renewed hopefulness. He must go away anxious to come back for the next meeting.

B. Use of word cards may provide success from the start.

Most non-readers hate books, or at least react with a hangdog, defeated air at the sight of a book. It is best, therefore, not to begin with books but with something which has no unfortunate associations.

A nucleus of sight words may be taught by use of cards bearing on one side a picture with a word under it and on the other the word only. Five or six cards are used to begin with. The child looks at the picture and says the word. When he has done this two or three times, shuffling the cards after each time, he turns the cards over and tries to say the words without the pictures. These cards can be made or secured from any school supply house. Words can also be taught by making a picture word book, which is a scrap book in which pictures are pasted with a word or phrase under each. If the child knows the alphabet, he can make a word book, putting new words on the proper pages according to first letters. Of course all words must be in print that is as like type as possible. A game called Reado is played like bingo to teach common words. It can be purchased or made.

The sight word cards, described on page 30, provide a method which has excellent results. The teacher can select from the 220 words a small group which she is sure the child will know or that can be taught very quickly. She will run over these and show him that he has something to start with or that he can learn words very easily. Her method will be to show the word, pronounce it, and have the child pronounce it as he looks at the word. In a few minutes, the child will confidently identify six or perhaps a dozen words. From this start the teacher can play the "word game" every day, reviewing the old words and teaching a few new ones. Every day she can show the child that he has a higher and higher record. Children who have been utterly discouraged about reading, attack this "word game" with great pleasure. They have found something at which they can "win." And a start is made at reversing the wrong attitude toward reading which would otherwise make progress practically impossible.

C. Making a book for the child gives him the pleasure of success.

Sometimes a good beginning is secured by making a book for the child. Use an ordinary blank notebook and print in it clearly. The first "story" may be something like this:

I am Tom Moore

I live in Johnstown

I go to the East School

The pupil can "read" several pages like this from memory. He may soon find that there are too many words for him to remember them all, but he will have learned some essential words before the interest wanes. With these, a transition can be made to a word card game or to the first pages of some pre-primer.

D. Show the child that he can read by teaching the words on the first page of an easy book.

If the child insists that he cannot learn to read, there is a way of showing him that he can. The teacher can use some attractive pre-primer which has a list of words, page by page, in the back. It should deal with pets or with something except the doings of very young children. The teacher should not show the first pages of the primer but instead turn to the word list. The first little story may be found to contain ten or twelve words. She can teach her pupil these words from the word list or from cards on which the words have been printed. The pupil, being older and more disciplined than a beginner, can learn these words as a job or "stunt," just to show that he can do it. The teacher can then open to the first page of the book and tell the pupil to go ahead and read. He will find to his surprise and pleasure that he can easily go through the story. Then the teacher can close the book, teach the next group of words and have some more reading. This method will give confidence and will help prove to the pupil that he can learn to read just as well as anyone.

E. Use strict vocabulary control on all material.

The non-reader is easily discouraged. He is very ready to quit when he meets strange words, for he has not learned how to get along in spite of vocabulary difficulty as others have done. So great care must be taken with the vocabulary of everything he reads. A modern school reader should be used which has a low vocabulary burden. Common words that he is to meet can be selected from the basic sight word cards and taught before reading is attempted. Nouns that are to be used can be taught beforehand. All this must be done to make the reading itself easy, successful, and pleasant. This will develop a desire to read, and desire will develop effort. With effort on the child's part, improvement is bound to follow.

F. Use material suited to the child's special interests.

If at all possible, we must put before the non-reader material that he wants to read. This, again, is to secure attention and effort on his part. Many children have developed some special interests such as in trains, airplanes,

Indians, cow-boys, pets, or the like. Easy material can be found on these subjects and on many others. The child's interests can usually be discovered through a friendly conversation, or by questioning. Some elaborate attempts have been made to take a complete "interest inventory" or remedial reading cases,[1] and this is an excellent thing to do, but should be attempted only after the child feels very much at home with the teacher; otherwise, true responses will not always be secured. If the remedial reading teacher learns enough about the child's school and home life, as we have suggested in the previous chapters, and if she and the child become rather close friends, she will have much of the information that she needs to guide her in the selection of material.

To adapt material to the student's interests, the teacher should be well acquainted with all the stories in the new primary readers. She will know where the airplane stories are, where the dog stories are, and the like. The Subject Index to Children's Readers, published by the American Library Association, will help in locating what is needed. The teacher can then use stories that the child will be anxious to read rather than just begin with a certain book and go through it. Of course, following a book gives the benefit of the vocabulary control by the author. If the teacher jumps from story to story for the sake of interest, she must see that there are not too many new words to teach.

---

[1] Copies of an Interest Inventory can be secured from Dr. Paul Witty, Northwestern University, Evanston, Illinois, or from the Reading Clinic, College of Education, University of Illinois, Urbana, Illinois.

G. Build up confidence by helping a great deal in all reading.

A common method in the teaching of reading is to help the reader very little and to insist that he struggle along by himself. The non-reader has tried this process for years and has found that he cannot do it. The remedial teacher must take quite a different tack. She will at first tell the child freely the words on which he hesitates and do so without delay so that the thread of the thought will not be broken. She is more concerned with his learning a different attitude toward reading than with his learning words. He must find reading a pleasure, and she must see that it is a pleasure. Occasionally, of course, she may suggest that the same word was met with in a previous sentence or had been on the word cards. But she will not do this as a piece of scolding. Occasionally, she will ask the child to guess at a word, but unless he can do so easily, she will tell the word and go on. In fact, remedial teaching will at first use very little of the pressure which has probably prevailed during the child's years of failure and discouragement. Instead, it will be frankly and constantly a process of helping the child get pleasure from reading. Drill will be introduced only in the spirit of a game and with caution so that the game will be a success.

H. Do not teach phonics until there is a good sight vocabulary.

Under the best of conditions, the teaching of phonics presents difficulties, and the conditions of the non-reader are far from the best. If he is taught phonics right away while he still lacks a sight vocabulary, he will start sounding out piece-meal those words which he should call off at half a glance. The only way to prevent this is to be sure that a considerable group of sight words are known before any teaching of phonics is begun. If a non-reader is of low mentality he is much more likely to use sight methods than to attempt sounding since slow learners generally find word analysis a most complicated process. For such cases, principles of sounding can be taught only very slowly and teaching of new words must continue to be by sight recognition. Many children are never able to use sounding but become passable readers by the slow building up of a large sight vocabulary of common words.

In the case of a bright child who, because of some special difficulty, has failed to learn to read until he is nine years old or more, phonics may be a short and quick solution to his whole difficulty. If he is mature enough to grasp phonics and to use phonics easily, he may start to read all sorts of books and to read a great deal. In one case a 13 year old boy changed in one year from a non-reader to a successful reader of fifth grade textbooks by learning for the first time how to sound out words. In such cases, the sight vocabulary will come as a natural result of much practice and because of the intelligence of the reader. These occasional cases should not lead one to generalize that phonics is the royal road to success in remedial reading. In most cases, phonics will not help much until there is maturity enough for the child to apply principles to new words and until there is determination enough on his part to do so.

III. Individual work with poor readers is just an adaptation of these methods that are used with non-readers.

Work with poor readers must apply the same principles we have set forth for work with non-readers. There must be (1) immediate success, (2) sight vocabulary, (3) interesting material, (4) much help, and (5) sounding when the (p.67) time is ripe for it. The adaptations to poor readers in intermediate and upper grades are discussed in Chapter VII.

CHAPTER VI

SPECIAL DISABILITIES

I. Special disabilities and bad habits appear both in non-readers and in poor readers.

The teacher working with reading deficiency cases will find a number of frequently recurring problems. It is not that cases fall into certain types which can be treated in certain definite ways, but that different children react to their difficulties at times in somewhat similar fashion. We shall discuss some of the more common of these reactions and suggest some things that may be done to correct them. Let us emphasize again, however, that though two children may do the same thing, they are still different children and will probably have to be treated differently. The remedial reading teacher is like the doctor, who, no matter how large his experience, always finds it necessary to watch the individual and adapt all methods to the new situation.

A. Poor attention, which is the hardest thing to combat, is of two kinds.

The most common fault of the poor reader is poor attention. It is often the reason why, through years of sitting with others in a large class, he has failed to learn to read. In fact, when one watches primary classes and notes how many children are paying no attention to the reading lesson, he wonders that so many children do learn to read. In all group remedial measures, poor attention is the greatest handicap. Even in individual work, it is a problem. The time for doing remedial work should be set with special regard to getting good attention. If the teacher must do the work outside school hours, the best time will be before school in the morning, because both pupil and teacher will be in best condition for attention. But even that time is not good if the sound of other children playing comes in the window. It is much better if work can be done during school hours, in a quiet room away from other children. A teacher can secure such time if she is relieved for a while by a special subject teacher or a substitute, or she may arrange work periods during which her presence in the room is not required.

The commonest difficulty is from "flighty" attention. The child's eyes wonder continually. He is distracted by the slightest sound or movement. It is hard to hold him to his tasks long enough for him to learn anything. Such a child becomes very exasperating. The teacher feels she is making no progress. She is tempted to become severe and to demand attention. The best solution in such cases is, of course, use of very interesting material—something that will, in itself, keep the child's mind upon reading. Such material may be very hard to find. Another recourse is to variety, changing the work a number of times during the period. This change is, in such cases, absolutely necessary. It may be necessary to start somtehing new every five minutes. Action or movement is another recourse, and that is one reason why card games work so well. The mere handling of the cards keeps attention. Sometimes, of course, sternness is necessary, but it must be used with caution. It will have no effect on some children, and a harmful effect on some others. At any rate it is certain the child will not learn to read unless his attention is on the reading. We must do everything we can to secure that attention.

A child with flighty attention needs to be given a thorough examination to see whether there is not some physical cause either in general health or sensory defect. His home needs to be investigated to see whether coffee drinking, late hours, over-stimulation, quarrelling or some other cause exists. Eyes need especially to be checked. Perhaps distaste of all reading work is a cause. If no such causes can be found, we must conclude that we have to deal with a temperamental or deep-seated habitual difficulty that will yield only to patient training.

The other type of poor attention may be called "half attention." The child will look at his book and seem to be paying good attention. He may even be following the story. Yet, every so often, he may make a remark which shows that part of his mind is elsewhere. And the work done at the next meeting may show that little was learned. Occasionally the child will fail to make progress with the basic sight word cards, and the reason can be found in the fact that he is only giving partial attention to the job. This situation is the more likely to arise the less interesting the material. It is also characteristic of bright children who are poor readers. They have become accustomed to getting along in school with "half attention," keeping their mind busy with affairs of their own concern. Ordinary school books are often matters of indifference to children who give only "half attention," and one is forced to find instead something in which the child is deeply interested. This may be impossible, and the reading of ordinary books may show little profit. One may have to be content with teaching by sheer repetition the common sight words, and hoping that later on some vital interest will develop which can secure full attention to reading.

B. Passiveness and resistance must be overcome.

Some children have developed, whether in school or out, the definite habit of not doing what they are told. As a result of years of experience, they have acquired a whole set of devices for getting out of doing things. Some of these children get tired very easily and lie over the desk in apparent exhaustion. Others get headaches very quickly, or have eyes which hurt when they are asked to read, even though no oculist has found any trouble with them. Some of these children are always full of bright thoughts that they must tell the teacher. Others love to start discussions about the story so that little or no reading gets done. It must be remembered that poor readers may be bright as well as dull, and the bright ones have found ways of their own of meeting the reading problem.

All types of resistance are best handled by kindly, gentle firmness. The child must learn that he cannot "get by" with his devices, though direct conflict is to be avoided. The teacher on her part must use some cleverness and often trick the child into doing his work. Of course, the best solution would be material which itself overcame all objection. Talks with the child will often reveal real interests or hobbies and a diligent search through modern primary books will locate something that may get better attention. The Subject Index to Children's Readers mentioned on page 57 will be useful.

C. Attention to the wrong parts of words is shown by reversals.

There has been much misunderstanding on the subject of so-called "reversals." These cases of miscalling words can sometimes be traced to reversing a letter as *dig* for *big,* sometimes to transposing letters as *stop* for *spot,* and sometimes to a reversing of the entire word as *saw* for *was.* The most often noticed type of reversals are confusions of one word with another. These are probably cases of mis-learning. In the beginning, the child confused the two words and so to speak, got them "twisted." In all subjects there are cases of learning of wrong associations. The remedy is to teach these associations correctly. Many of these sets of often confused words are found in the basic sight vocabulary. When two words have become "twisted," as we say, the cards for the two words can be placed one above the other and the child can be shown the difference. Printing the words one above the other or having the pupil print them will have the same effect. The other type of reversal seems to be a persistent habit of calling a word some other word that begins with some prominent letter in the word, often the one on the end. These are not cases of consistent eye movements in the wrong direction, as can be proved by photographing the eyes. They are really cases in which the eyes do a great deal of wandering back and forth along the line as they do with practically all immature readers. They are also cases of never having learned the habit of paying special attention to how a word begins. A beginning reader is likely to notice any prominent letter, such as a tall letter at any point, a dotted *i* or a rounded *o.* Gradually we train the child to notice the left end of a word, especially the initial letter, which is a cue to rapid recognition. But many poor readers have never learned this habit and are confused or misled by prominent letters other than the initial.

When we find a child who miscalls words through notic-ing the wrong parts, we can remedy the situation by systematically teaching the noticing of how words begin. Whenever there is a mistake we ask, ''How does the word begin?'' This means, of course, ''With what *sound* does the word begin?,'' since we do not want the names of letters to be given. As an exercise, it is a good plan to have a child go through part of a story, not reading but sounding the beginning letter of each word. This to produce the habit of noticing beginnings. The teaching of phonics is always an excellent way of securing habits that overcome reversals because words are always sounded from left to right. If we have a very strong case of eye wandering, we can help it by having the child point for a time to each word as he reads it. Another device is to have him count the words he has read, thus causing him to follow the line from left to right. But with all these devices, we should use such very easy reading matter that the story itself keeps the child going along the line steadily and freely.

A great deal too much has been made of reversals in reading. The child who miscalls words this way has either bad habits or has failed to acquire good ones. We merely go ahead and teach him how to read correctly. There is much talk about reversals and left-handedness. Both of these may be found together and they may be closely related. The left-handed child follows his hand with his eye, and his hand goes most easily from right to left. Thus he may more readily make eye movements from right to left and he may more readily notice the right end of words. But we must remember that the world is full of left-handed people who learned to read without the least trouble. There are also languages in which right-handed people have to learn to read from right to left and other languages where people learn to read from top to bottom of the page. Teaching reading is teaching habits, so let us teach the right habits as efficiently and as rapidly as possible.

D. Over-emphasis on certain methods of attack may have produced certain bad habits in reading.

Some of the bad habits we shall mention are simply cases of too much emphasis upon what would otherwise be a good habit. The three habits of attack in reading should all be present and should all work together, without undue prominence of any single one. The child should recognize by sight, he should guess words from context, and he should use sounding. To do any one of these three to the exclusion of the other two makes a poor reader. Ordinarily children develop these three methods together or in such a way that all work together to the best advantage. Sometimes children fail to learn one of these methods and as a result are handicapped in reading. Remedial work consists in restoring the balance, as we shall see in the following paragraphs.

1. A most general handicap is lacking of all knowledge of sounding.

It may almost be taken for granted that no poor reader is capable of sounding out words for himself. Many of these children were slow in development, and when they were taught sounding in the primary grades they were mentally too young to grasp the subject. For them the teaching of sounding came too early. Then the probabilities are that the schools, having taught phonics once, paid little further regular attention to it, instead of repeatedly reteaching it grade after grade. As a result, the poor reader never did learn phonics. He has therefore had to rely on what sight words he could pick up and on the guessing he could do.

It may, therefore, be accepted that all remedial reading includes the teaching of phonics. The details of this work appear in the next chapter. We may here make the explanation, however, that there are many poor readers who will never learn phonics. First of all, they may lack the mentality or the application required for the work. Sounding means forming generalizations and using them in new situations. Some children have not attained or will not attain the mental maturity that such work requires. Second, some children of fully adequate intelligence are especially handicapped in the auditory abilities which sounding requires. These children simply cannot separate the sound of a word into its parts. They cannot hear similarities of sounds. Or they cannot blend separate sounds into words. This does not mean that they may not become good readers. If their other abilities are good, they may learn many thousands of words as sight words by the process of being told them repeatedly. Many more children progress in reading this way than we have any idea of.

2. Some children have a habit of trying to sound out all the words they meet.

The occasional poor reader who desperately attempts to sound out even the simplest words is not a case of too much phonic teaching as is often claimed. Instead, he is an unusual result of our usual methods of teaching reading. The first year is customarily devoted to sight learning. Children are told what the words say and should associate the sound with the word picture. Some children, however, go through this sight period without getting any sight vocabulary. They either memorize the stories or are entirely indifferent. In the second year, intensive work with phonics is often begun. At this time some of these children begin to work at reading and somehow get the notion that every word is to be sounded. They do not look at the word as a whole but always at the first letter, second letter, and so on. We should not blame the teaching of phonics for this situation, but rather our failure to assure a sight vocabulary before the phonic attack was emphasized.

The best treatment for these cases is insistance that the common words be given only a single glance. Sight words must be "flashed," giving no opportunity for more than one look. Flash cards of any kind may be used but it is much better to use cards on which the words are printed in book size type. A tachistocope such as comes with the Durell materials (see page 140) will also serve. The child will at first be bewildered and guess wildly, but he will soon develop the method of recognizing words by general appearance. He will, in fact, be surprised that words can be recognized that way. He should be taught the common words by this method, eliminating all sounding for the time being. Even in reading, he should be told a word before he has time to sound it. When a sight vocabulary has finally been established, his sounding habits can be checked over and corrected if necessary. He will then be well prepared for making progress by his own efforts.

3. Some children have the habit of word calling without attention to sense.

Some children may have a fairly good sight vocabulary and may even be able to sound out some words and yet read word after word without paying any attention to sentence meaning. This is not, as is often thought, the product of any particular method of teaching. All methods must teach words because everyone reads by reading words. The explanation is often clear when we note the type of child who does this word calling. Usually he is distinctly indifferent to the subject matter of school books. The "reading history" of such a child is usually sufficient to account for word calling. He has never cared what a book said, but he was told that he had to read. He found that if he said all the words correctly he was praised. Therefore he got the idea that reading means saying the words. Therefore he says the words and calls it reading. A strong factor leading to word calling is that school books are not only uninteresting to many children but are also too hard for them. There are too many hard words and the sentences are too long. After a pupil has struggled through a sentence of twenty to thirty words, many of them long and difficult, he naturally has little idea what it was all about. At times, we even find that some children who recognize words quite freely still have little idea that reading is supposed to be a process of thought getting. If only all teaching of beginning reading made the children understand that word pronouncing is not enough. If it always made clear that the meaning, the idea, is the thing, we would not have cases of word-callers to contend with.

The best remedy for word calling is the use of simple material in which the child has a vital interest. Give him easy stories that have suspense, and notice how he at once pays attention to thought. The meaning of the sentences will be bound to register in the child's mind. Such material is hard to find because the child's interests may be physical and social only. Hobbies may be discovered and encouraged so that a demand for some kind of reading may arise. If we give the child thought that has appeal, expressed in easy words and sentences, mere word calling will stop.

Another remedy for word calling is continual insistence that the child answer questions about or explain what he has read. Thus he may get the idea that reading is a process of understanding. Constant practice will be necessary before he gets the habit of understanding and thinking about what is read, since mere saying of words is an easier process. Word books which demand understanding will help if enough practice is given. No long standing habit can be changed except by a good deal of time and effort. If, from the beginning of reading in school, there had been constant discussion of reading matter by all children, there would be no trouble with word calling later.

One special type of word calling may be mentioned. Occasionally a child of quite low mentality will have a special ability for learning separate words by sight. He will be able, therefore, to call off these words one after another in reading matter, but without the least understanding. In such a case one may be astounded by the fluent word calling with apparently no comprehension, the reason being, of course, in the lack of intelligence to understand with. Yet even these children can be helped by use of questions on the reading matter.

4. Some children have the habit of "making up" what they "read" either from picture reading or from context or imagination.

Some children read rather fluently and smoothly but one is astonished to find they have left out words or parts of sentences or have put in much that simply is not there. These children are intelligent and imaginative and have acquired the habit of "interpreting" the page rather than reading it. They may get most of the story from the pictures and then say it in a form that more or less corresponds with the printed matter. Or the child may have developed skill in reading part of the context and filling in the balance from imagination. The child finds this quite satisfactory for his purposes and gets along very well so long as silent reading is expected. He can answer questions about a story and can even do work books and answer questions in content subjects. Some of them read many library books. All teachers know of some such case and will often say, "He can read perfectly well when he reads to himself, but cannot do very well when asked to read orally."

Children who are handicapped by too much guessing or imagining can simply be required to read aloud and to read word for word. It may be found that they are short on sight vocabulary, and the basic words may be taught. It will certainly be found that they cannot sound out new words, for they have never thought that they had to. In that case sounding can be taught. It is important, however, that these children become conscious that they are doing a poor kind of reading and that they try to change this habit.

5. Some children make no attempt to guess from context or to skip and go on.

Some poor readers seem to have the idea that they must read one word after the other and that if they come to one which they do not know, all further progress is impossbile. No one seems ever to have told them to go on and read the rest of the sentence and thus keep up with the story regardless of unknown words. It may even be that some teacher told them it was wrong to "skip and go on." Teachers do say that to the careless type of reader.

Most children learn on their own account to read in spite of unknown words. Those who do not learn this are condemned to be poor readers, for obviously, a child who is going to stop reading when he meets a strange word is not going to read very much in school or out.

"To skip and go on" may mean no attempt to guess the meaning of the unknown word. "To guess from context" means to try to tell what the word means. The two processes are closely related but both are needed if a child is to teach himself through his reading. He must go on past the unknown word and get the larger ideas but he must also learn new words by use of context. A poor reader needs to be shown how to use both these methods. He needs to be told "Go on and read the rest of the sentence" and he needs to be asked "Now what do you think the word means?" He will be delighted to find he can make progress in both these ways, and he will begin to be in part his own teacher from that time on. Care must be taken, however, to see that the child knows enough words to be able to apply these methods successfully. If there are a number of unknown words in one sentence, no "reading on" or "guessing from context" is possible. The teacher can help if necessary, by telling all of the hard words but one.

CHAPTER VII

POOR READERS IN MIDDLE AND UPPER GRADES

I. Poor Readers in the middle and upper grades must be given books that are at their real reading level.

Parents and some teachers think that, even though a child is only a second grade reader, he can be given a fifth grade book and learn to read from it. All over the country teachers are therefore trying to teach poor readers out of books that are too hard for them. Time should have proved the uselessness of this endeavor. The reasons for it are simple. First, the child's attitude is one of failure and hopelessness instead of one of confidence and eagerness. Second, there is little hope of learning sight vocabulary because the page presents a constant procession of new words, that is, words unknown to the child. The middle grade book does not limit vocabulary or provide the frequent repetitions as primary books do. The common words are there, it is true, but they are lost in the forest of unknown words. Third, new words cannot be guessed from context because the number of strange words keeps the child from getting or holding the train of thought. Therefore, trying to teach a child to read from a book that is too hard for him is almost an impossible task. He needs to be put back on books of his true reading level, and to work up from there.

We have assumed that most non-readers in the primary grades can use the material usually intended for beginners. Pre-primers and primers can be found which deal with animals or with children's activities that are not too far away from the interests even of the eight year old. In the middle grades, however, we find children who may still be such poor readers that they cannot deal with more than primers. These children are nine years old or more. They are well developed in their sports and play life and may be working in the adult world after school hours. To secure easy reading material suitable for them is a problem indeed.

A. These children cannot use "baby stuff."

Big capable boys and girls cannot be asked to read about Jip and Jerry on their scooters or about other things suitable for six year olds. Yet, their reading ability may be at the primer level. Here is one of the acute problems of all remedial reading. Our chief recourse is to search through first grade material for things which deal not with the activities of little children but with the world about us. Anything at first grade reading level will do so long as there is no mention of small children in it. At present, some of the best material is in the Unit Lesson Reading Series.[1] These are cheap booklets, well illustrated, written at levels from the first grade on up. The grading is not marked on the book. Other publishers have little social science books about farm animals, transportation, food, houses, etc., which are at low reading level but will interest older children. The Weekly Reader for Primary Grades may also be used when it so happens that no mention of small youngsters is contained in it. Publishers are more and more beginning to meet the demand for books of middle grade maturity but primary difficulty. However, the problem of easy enough material for these older poor readers is

---

[1] Inquire of the American Education Press, Columbus, Ohio. They also publish the *Weekly Reader*.

still acute.   Each teacher can watch advertisements and book exhibits and accumulate a collection of this type of book.

B. Some poor readers of this level are not appealed to by stories.

It is usually assumed that we can reach any child through interesting stories. But many poor readers in the middle and upper grades are boys who are very factually minded and who insist they do not like to read stories. This immediately discards a great deal of the material on which the remedial reading teacher usually depends. She must then discover hobbies or subjects of special interest to the individual, such as mechanics or aviation or football, and start hunting for easy material on the desired subject. If she cannot find easy material that will appeal to the child, find material which is of vital interest to him, and help him to struggle through it by telling him a great many of the words. For instance, she can help a boy who is interested only in athletics to struggle through the sport page. She can help a boy who is fascinated by automobiles to work through a book about making or driving cars. This follows the principle that where interest is great enough, we can keep a child going in spite of difficulties.

C. For some children, special reading material should be made.

Sometimes it is advisable to prepare with the child a book of his own. The process is the same as with a primary experience chart. Have the child tell you his experiences or likes or desires and put them down in simple sentences, in print form. Then have him read the pages back to you. Try to use the same words over and over. Make a book of the pages so that they can be read over and over and used as a sort of dictionary. The child can remember having seen a word before and look back and find it. For the child to be helped by memory, each page should be a definite interesting unit, such as *My Dog, My Visit to the Country, What I Want to Be, An Accident I had,* and so on.

At times, the poor reader can be greatly helped by use of the typewriter. He can copy words or a simple story and thus be compelled to look carefully and to pay attention to the left end of a word first.

II. Poor readers in the middle and upper grades have certain typical difficulties.

We have already described the approach with non-readers. We shall now deal, not with those who cannot read at all, but with those who may be classed as poor readers. That is, they may be able satisfactorily to read primers and first readers or even something more advanced, but they are still more than one year and maybe two years or more behind in reading. With these poor readers we find the same attitude problems that we have discussed as characteristic of non-readers. They have a strong sense of failure. They may show it by passiveness or lethargy, or they may try to cover it up by bravado and boastfulness. Many will insist loudly that they can "read all right." There is also likely to be distinct antagonism to books. We meet this situation chiefly by giving very easy, interesting books, as described in the last section. We also meet it with hearty friendliness and an utter absence of scolding or blame.

We take the attitude that here is a problem and we are both going to attack it and solve it.

A. Inadequate sight vocabulary is common.

Poor readers in the middle grades and later know some words by sight but generally not enough for them to read fluently. The situation can be observed by just having the pupil read some easy material or read the beginning paragraph of the Gray Oral Reading Paragraphs. Either method will give a general impression of just how poor the sight vocabulary is. A more exact measure is given by use of the Dolch-Gray Word Recognition tests, of which there are three, 25 words each. This enables a test on 75 common words. A still more complete diagnosis can be made by use of the basic sight word cards.[2] These present, in primer type, the 220 most useful "service words," that is, prepositions, conjunctions, pronouns, verbs, adverbs and adjectives. (See Appendix B.) It has often been found that fully a third of fourth graders and many fifth and sixth graders are such poor readers that they do not recognize instantly all of these 220 words. The poor reader's knowledge of them is tested by the method explained in Appendix C. After the teacher has tested out the children with the cards, she may get a set for each child who needs help.

The teacher may teach each poor reader herself, but children of these grades are old enough to help one another in this word game. The poor reader is called the player, and to each player is assigned a good reader, who is called

---

[2] See "The First Step in Remedial Reading," E. W. Dolch, *Elementary School Journal*, Chicago, December, 1936.

a helper. These pairs play the game at a time and place when they will not disturb others or be disturbed, though a large number of pairs can be working in a room at the same time. The player turns over the cards himself as fast as he can, calling each one and handing it to the helper. If the card is called right the helper puts it on the desk; if not, he keeps it in his hand. When all cards have been called, the player counts the number right and puts the result down on a chart. Then the helper hands back the cards he has, one at a time, telling what the right word is. The player repeats each word after him. The right and the wrong cards are then shuffled together ready for the next attempt. In the case of a very poor reader, to use the whole pack will cause too much discouragement. Instead, only the easiest words should be selected and new, unknown words should be *introduced gradually*.

It will be seen that two purposes are served by the word game. First, the child learns to recognize words he did not know before. Second, he is speeded up in his recognizing of the known words. This speeding up is important in making his ordinary reading faster and easier, since the basic sight words make up more than half of all his reading matter.

Children may know all the basic sight words and still have a poor sight vocabulary, because by fourth grade a child should know several thousand words instantly by sight. A remedy for this defect is suggested in the next section.

B. A slow laborious reading habit needs to be corrected.

Practically all poor readers in the middle grades have always been slow laborious readers, and they never expect to be anything else. Even if they do know many words, they recognize them slowly and drag out their sentences to an extent that it is small wonder their comprehension is poor.

These children need to realize that they can read faster, and they must learn to expect to read faster. To put this point across, the teacher will go back to some material so easy that the child is sure to know all the words. She will time him as he reads for several minutes. She may discover that his rate is only sixty words per minute, or one word per second, which is the speed suitable for the end of the first grade or it may be 90 to 100 words per minute yet still too slow for smooth, easy comprehension. She will then point out that this speed is far too slow and have the child read the very same thing over again, urging him to go faster, and keeping time. He will improve but not enough. Then to show him how well he can do, she may have him read the same section, with timing, every day for a week. He may double his first record and will for the first time have had the experience of running his eyes rapidly ahead as he follows the thought. This will not guarantee that he will always read with this greater speed. Only much practice with easy material will do that. But *this device of re-reading* will convince him he *can* go fast, and he will then try to do so. The same purpose can be secured if the child is allowed to take home stories or books he has already read so that he can read them over to members of his family. Parents must be instructed to applaud his efforts so that this device will give continued encouragement.

Another device to speed up slow readers is *pushing with a card*. The teacher holds a card that extends across the page, and moves it down the page, a line at a time. She counts a certain number of seconds before each movement of the card. If there are eight words on a line, and the count is five seconds, the speed will be eight words in five seconds or 96 words a minute. If the count is four seconds per line, the speed will be 120 words per minute; if three seconds per line, 160 words per minute, and so on, provided of course that each line has an average of eight words. From this method let the child read ahead on the easy parts if he can, but sets a minimum speed for the whole. Keeping ahead of the card is an interesting game that also increases speed of reading. This method of pushing should be compared with the use of the metronoscope, as discussed in Appendix F.

A large group of poor readers, or even a whole room, may be speeded up in reading by a *"rapid reading period."* In the first place, school authorities can recognize that children should read rapidly and that the only way to learn to read rapidly is to read rapidly. Reading slowly, as is characteristic of most textbook reading, does not teach children to read fast. That is why a special period must be assigned for rapid reading if rapid reading is desired. In the second place, no child can read rapidly unless he has an easy enough book to read. A hard book means slow reading, and slow reading does not teach fast reading. Therefore, school authorities must recognize that a rapid reading period demands easy books, and this means some books easy enough for the poorest reader. A rapid reading period in the middle grades therefore requires books of difficulty that ranges from the first grade up. The various new series without grade markings make this possible, and each room can be supplied with one series each, of all the new readers which are not marked for grade. Finally, if rapid reading is really desired, a special period is needed for it every day and not once a week, as is sometimes arranged. No deep set habits can be changed by practice once a week. Twenty minutes a day is minimum, and thirty minutes is much better.

In this rapid reading period, each child is required to choose some book he likes and to read it to himself steadily for the entire period. The teacher circulates about the room to see that everybody is busy. She may sit beside a child and have him read a little to her in a low voice to see if the book is suitable for him. There is no check on comprehension because that factor is being left out for the time being for the sake of speed. Likewise, no normal child will read steadily in a book without comprehending something of what he is reading. In other reading done during the day there is plenty of chance to stress accurate and complete comprehension.

Even without a rapid reading period there is great need for a room library containing very easy books. Poor readers can read them at odd moments or take them home to read. The poor reader must read easy books if he is to improve. Hard books merely maintain and increase the habit of slow reading.

C. Practically all poor readers need to be taught sounding.

Sometimes the poor readers in the middle grades and later do have some imperfect method of sounding attack on new words. It is possible to have them try to work out strange words and by watching how they do it, discover which elements of sounding they know and which they do not. Use of the Dolch-Gray Word Attack tests will help in determining what they know and what they do not know. In making this diagnosis the teacher should watch for ignorance or errors in the ten following elements or "steps in Sounding":

1. Single consonant sounds.
2. Consonant digraphs.
3. Short sounds of vowels.
4. Long sounds of vowels.
5. Final *e* rule.
6. Double vowels.
7. Diphthongs.
8. Soft *c* and *g*.
9. Number of syllables.
10. Division into syllables.

These steps in sounding are roughly in order of use or difficulty and they furnish a convenient method of noting the child's progress in sounding. It will often be found, for instance, that one or two of the consonant sounds may be unknown, or that a certain consonant digraph is mispronounced, or that all vowels are called short or that all are called long, or that some of the diphthongs are unknown. As each definite defect is located, record should be made. Then as occasion offers the particular elements needed can be definitely taught. Of course errors in syllabication cannot be emphasized until the separate elements are well known.

For remedial cases, sounding shall be connected as much as possible with the reading. The method is for the teacher to note from the record of "Steps in Sounding" what the child needs next, keep it in mind as he reads to her, and seize upon the teaching opportunities furnished by the text. Very often sound words fitting the next principle to be taught will occur close together. Then they can be pointed out or printed above one another and the child helped to see for himself the similarity in letters and sounding. Sounding should also be taught in conjunction with guessing from context. The child should guess what he thinks the word is and verify his guess by sounding. Or he may sound out part of the word and then, from suggestion of context, guess the rest. Sounding is not a science for itself to be learned separately and then applied to reading. It is only a tool for word recognition. The sounding, whether of part or all of the word, is intended to lead the pupil to think of a word that is already familiar in sound and meaning. If a word is sounded out and is not recognized as already known, it should be looked up in a dictionary. One should not try to learn the sound of entirely new words from sounding out, as there is too much chance of error, especially because of not being sure where the accent should be. If sounding does not bring a familiar word to mind, look in the dictionary for both correct sound and correct meaning of the new word.

If the child seems to have very little knowledge of phonics, and the teacher has his full coöperation, the simplest course is to make a systematic review of the chief elements of sounding. Here again is a piece of work which may be done individually or with a group or class. In fact, it is a good thing to review sounding at the beginning of each grade school year. The good readers will not be harmed by it, and all the poor and average readers will benefit.

A consonant such as *t* is taught by first listing, one beneath the other, familiar words beginning with the sound of *t*. The teacher pronounces the words, emphasizing somewhat the initial sound, while the child listens for "how the words begin." The child then reads each word, trying to "hear" the beginning sound. Then the teacher may list similarly familiar words ending with the sound of *t*, and again pronounce the words, stressing the final sound a little. The child will read the words and listen to the sound of the last letter. Then the teacher will print new words that begin or end in *t* and let the child have practice in using the *t* sound. Some groups such as we have mentioned follow:

| to | try | hat | sit |
| ten | tell | met | but |

The other phonetic elements are taught by a similar process of word comparison. All phonetic principles are generalizations, and the pupil should make these generalizations himself from words he knows. He is then much more likely to use the principles on new words. After the vowel principles are taught by word comparison, children can be given practice in applying these by finding on a page of easy reading words having vowel sounds similar to the following key words:

Short vowels: bat, bet, bit, but, hot.

Final *e*: came, home, time.

    (Final *e* after *e* or *u* too rare to need teaching.)

Double vowels: boat, meat, feet.

Diphthongs: house, cow, toot.

The teaching of phonograms (vowel and consonant combinations) is not recommended as they are of little usefulness in pronouncing the polysyllables that are the chief sounding problem in all reading. When we divide long words into syllables, most of these syllables begin with consonants, not with vowels as do the "common phonograms." Anyone can check this for himself. Divide long words into syllables and note that practically all of them, except endings such as -ing, -ed, or -er, begin with consonants. Then note that all phonograms usually taught in phonic lessons begin with vowels. Thus these phonograms could not be of much help with polysyllables.[3]

If the single elements are known, it is usually necessary to teach syllabication, a much neglected subject. The usual principles for syllabication follow:

1. There are as many syllables as there are vowels (with the exception ordinarily of double vowels and final e).

2. Consonants usually go with the following vowel if they can be pronounced with it.

3. Division comes between double consonants.

4. Prefixes and suffixes remain separate syllables.

5. Closed syllables are usually short and open ones long, if accented.

After division is taught, the sounds of syllables are worked out, using consonants and consonant digraphs as already learned. A great deal of practice is needed before syllabication is mastered. And, as stated above, if the word arrived at is not a familiar one, it is best to go to the dic-

---

[3] See "Phonics and Polysyllables," E. W. Dolch, *Elementary English Review*, April, 1938.) Many devices for teaching sounding may be found in a little book entitled "Reading Aids Through the Grades, 225 Remedial Reading Activities," by Russell, Karp & Kelly (Bureau of Publications, Teachers College, New York.

tionary to find the exact sounding. Finally, as suggested on page 68, some children are handicapped in the use of phonics and may never have much success. They may, however, like all children, continually build up an ever increasing sight vocabulary by being told repeatedly. The ordinary child builds up his sight vocabulary by sounding.

To concentrate attention on sounding, children may individually or in a group use a sounding work book. Those by Marjorie Hardy are the most simple. Those by Stone[4] are suitable if the children have enough sight vocabulary to read the instruction sentences. Some children respond well to a work book and find it interesting and profitable. Some children cannot work alone and merely waste time. The teacher must experiment with these books to discover when and how to use them. Work books are chiefly valuable to bring points to a child's attention. Then there must be much application in reading. A single work book cannot be trusted alone to build habits because a habit necessarily demands more practice than one such book can give.

D. Comprehension may be increased to some extent.

Poor readers seldom comprehend as well as we should like them to. One reason for this is that much of the poor reader's attention is taken up with word difficulties. Attention to details of words naturally detracts from attention to meaning of the sentences. Slow word recognition also slows up the process so that the child takes a long time to read a sentence and he therefore loses track of the sentence idea. Another reason for poor comprehension is that poor readers are habitually more or less indifferent to the mean-

---

[4] *Eye and Ear Fun.* Clarence Stone. Webster Publishing Co., St. Louis, Mo. Three workbooks of increasing difficulty.

ing of what they read. Reading has always been hard and nearly always uninteresting. Teachers have either emphasized mere pronouncing or they have been obviously expecting poor results. Reading has just been something to get over with.

In this situation, the best way to get increased comprehension is to provide easier and more interesting reading matter. Easier reading matter naturally is found more interesting because it is better understood. Then if the material has plot and suspense, or if it deals with things that appeal to the child, there is an immediate "pull" on the attention and the comprehension increases. Attention and effort naturally produce comprehension. Not all reading materials can be easy and interesting, however. School books must be taken as they come. Therefore the child needs the habit of getting all he can from what he reads, even though it may not greatly interest him. He must get the habit of "digging out" meaning. This habit may be developed through sympathetic questioning by the teacher and discussion *by the poor readers* of what is read. Unfortunately the bright children in a class dominate the situation and embarrass the others into silence. To avoid this the poor readers need to be in a group of their own. Of course discussion of content uses time in talking instead of reading but this is necessary if comprehension is to be increased.

Pressure for more adequate comprehension can also be made through use of work books. The definite questions in the work book require definite answers, and the child discovers that reading carefully once may save re-reading several times. There must however be much time spent on work books if improvement is to be expected. Change in habits take time and effort. The work book should be independent of readers if possible. It is very clumsy and confusing for the poor reader to refer back and forth from work book to text or text to work book.

The great caution for use of work books is that they must be easy enough for the child to read. If he is two years below his grade in reading, the reading matter in the work book must be two years below. Unless the work book is fully easy enough, its use does more harm than good. It becomes not an exercise in reading and comprehension but a guessing contest, and makes the child think more than ever that reading is a puzzle and a nuisance. Just because teachers so seldom get work books that are easy enough, there is a general sentiment against their use. This is unfortunate. It is not the fault of the work book idea. If we get easy work books the children are sure to learn that reading is thought getting. And their process of thought getting will be improved. The adaptation of work books to different levels of reading ability is another reason for their being self sufficient or independent of readers. Of course, if a child is being given individual work, he can be given an easier reader with a work book dependent on it.

We have spoken of general comprehension and not of special study skills. The latter will be discussed in a following chapter which deals with remedial work in the high school because there the special skills are greatly emphasized. This does not mean that certain of these skills should not be taught in the grades also.

E. Interests for future reading should be developed.

Remedial work in school is just a beginning. If, after the poor readers leave school, they do not read, either all progress will cease or ground will be lost by mere lack of practice. These individuals therefore need interests in reading as well as the minimum ability we can develop in the limited school time. Practically this means bringing to their attention a type of reading matter that they will want to continue reading. For some this will be the story of excitement or adventure, even the detective story if need be. If as adults, they should read detective stories, they will maintain or increase their reading ability for use on other kinds of reading when the occasion arises. For some individuals, the western story is the kind that will keep them reading. For some, the magazines on inventions and mechanics will offer a continuing interest. For some, it may be the sport page. For some, it may be the newspaper pages of bargains. All of these "continuing interests" are means of keeping these poor readers readers. Only if they read will they learn to read better. So it is imperative to discover and to develop interests for future reading.

CHAPTER VIII

REMEDIAL READING IN HIGH SCHOOLS

I. Departmentalized Work brings a radically different situation.

In the grade schools, the room teacher feels the responsibility for the poor reader's school life and work, or the building principal assigns that responsibility to a remedial teacher. In the high school, work is departmentalized and each teacher tends to be responsible only for a child's work in a single subject. This is one of the reasons that little progress has been made until recently in helping the poor reader in high school. A second reason is that poor readers were so repeatedly failed that they never got to the high school level. A third reason has been that poor readers who did get to high school "failed out" because of their inability to do the work in some of the "book subjects." Now all of these situations have changed. A higher compulsory education limit keeps the poor readers in school longer. A policy of promotion planned to do away with too great over-ageness permits poor readers to go on into high school. And the high school principals are assuming a responsibility for the children's mental health, general development, and vocational future which makes them recognize poor readers as a problem which cannot be left to a goup of subject-matter teachers, each interested only in a single field of content.

The methods of remedial reading in the grades apply also to the same type of work in high school, but the administrative problems are somewhat different. We shall point out therefore special methods which apply to high school work.

II. Modification of the regular English course is the direct attack on the reading situation in high school.

Reading difficulty in high school hinders the work, not of a few students only, but in many schools of as many as a third or more. This is caused by the fact that reading matter assigned to high school students is of about the same nature as that found in the course of study some decades ago, whereas more and more poor readers are reaching the high school level. In the English work especially, there is now a very great gap between the reading difficulty of material and the reading ability of great numbers of students. The only sensible thing is to lessen that gap. After having done so, we can consider the problem of the smaller number of students who are still unable to do their work.

A. Easier required readings are being used.

On the earnest demand of many English teachers, publishers are now issuing for Junior High Schools and for the first year or two of Senior High Schools, volumes of selections which are distinctly easier reading than many books heretofore used. Contemporary American writing is especially featured. Work by living poets and living prose writers is generally found to be on subjects that interest modern students and in a vocabulary the student can understand. Such modern writing has a more simple and direct style, yet it may nonetheless have a true literary quality. Contemporary short stories and plays are especially emphasized. It is felt that there will be time enough in the later high school years and in college for students to become acquainted with the classics of England and of previous centuries. A teacher can learn of these new books of selections for class reading by inquiring of the publishers. Some of them will be found listed in a Bulletin of the University of Illinois, Vol. XXXV, No. 83, June 14, 1938, entitled "Suggestions for Improving Instruction in English."

B. Vocabulary building is emphasized as a practical utility.

When classics of a former age are emphasized with the younger children in high school, it is difficult to make vocabulary study vital because the new words are likely to be either distinctly literary or archaic. When more modern writings are used, we can rightly say that the new words met with are to be found in the reading of modern books and magazines and are in many cases in common use by educated people. Thus even the poorest readers are stimulated to try to learn new words.

Word study should be at all times, and with all children, a game rather than a task. The origin, the form, the particular meaning of words is a subject of absorbing interest. Oral discussion of new words creates spontaneous interest in the classroom. Children like to report having heard or seen outside of school some of the new words met in reading. After the children have tried to work out a meaning from content or from similarity with known words, they will find it fun to check by use of the dictionary. Sources of words and the interesting families of words such as *telegraph, telephone, phonograph,* etc., get real attention and enlarge vocabulary. Interest in words and pride in a larger vocabulary are all that is needed to get results.

C. Sounding can be taught to all.

All courses in high school present new words which the student should be able to sound out for himself. Few students are able satisfactorily to work out for themselves these new words. The English teacher can profitably review syllabication and sounding every year. The most direct attack on sounding is through study of the pronounciation of hard words selected from the materials read. The teacher can give the full pronunciation and the class can then check this to see how the rules for syllabication and sounding are or are not followed. Then the word should be looked up in the dictionary to further check on the sounding. The word itself and not the respelling in the dictionary is to be emphasized lest the children get the wrong visual picture. But the dictionary respelling will be used until the children become skillful in making sure just how a word is sounded correctly. This does not mean memorizing diacritical marks. These marks, if learned at all, should be learned incidentally through their use in these exercises.

All high school subjects will have new words. Most teachers teach these as sight words, telling the class the pronunciation as they look at the word. They would do better, however, at least to pronounce syllable by syllable and it would be still better to do as suggested above, help the pupils to work out the word themselves by applying the rules for syllabication and the general principles of phonics. Any content subject, history, science, or what not, should help the pupils to learn to work out words as they will have to work them out in later life when there is no one to tell them the pronunciation.

D. Classroom work in intensive reading can also give training in comprehension for poor readers.

Class room work in intensive reading should not emphasize merely work with words. Even more attention should be given to training in thoughtful reading. The thoughtful reader realizes the full import of what he reads and makes some reflection upon it. Our questions in class should therefore first make sure that the children *understand* what they have read, especially in the case of non-fiction. Most of the children's reading is story reading where all they need to get is the thread of events. When, instead, we ask them to read description or explanation, they do not always get the real thought. In addition to strange words, long sentences with qualifying clauses give special trouble, and one will often find through questioning that the qualifications were not noticed and that a quite distorted idea resulted. In intensive reading, questions should therefore first be directed towards more complete and more accurate understanding.

Questions in the class period should also encourage *reaction* to what is read. Is the idea clearly expressed? Is the scene sufficiently described? Is the person attractive or un-attractive? Is the statement right or wrong? It must be emphasized that careful reading means thinking about what is read. When the typical high school class is directed to read a part of a selection, they will finish and sit looking at the teacher, waiting for her to ask something. Instead, just as soon as the reading is finished, hands should go up. There should be questions that the pupils wish to ask, comments that they want to make, etc. They should expect to think and to say something about anything that they read. That is what reading is for, to give us something to think about. The teacher may encourage this thinking by giving questions beforehand, but this device should be only a temporary one and should soon become unnecessary, the pupils thinking of their own questions or comments as they read. Habits both of comprehension and of reaction to reading matter should be practiced in the English class regardless of the content of the book or the other aims of the course. They should be practiced in all other classes likewise. They can be practiced outside also if we make suitable home assignments.

E. Outside reading permits of the most helpful modification of the English course to improve reading.

English has always included outside reading, usually from the titles on a book list. The purpose has been to encourage extensive reading and to give acquaintance with more books than can be dealt with in the class. The practice of having outside reading should be continued, but with certain changes to suit the lower reading ability of incoming students and the greater emphasis that must therefore be placed upon reading.

1. Extensive reading habits are very different from the habits of intensive reading described above.

The teaching of English has often made the great mistake of assuming that all reading should be of the slow, analytic type that is usual in class room work. This is far from being the case. Adults need only to consider their own reading to discover that they have two very different reading habits. One, the careful reading habit just described, is used in reading contracts, directions, articles or books in the reader's own field of work, or other kinds of material where complete comprehension is necessary. Yet very little of what we read requires or deserves this kind of very careful reading. Usually we use our extensive reading habit. With newspapers, magazines, and with most books, we go as rapidly as we can while comprehending as much as suits our purpose. Our purpose is usually one of two: first, to know what the material is about or to get the general idea, as we would say, and second, to locate some fact or information. In either case there is rapid reading with just enough comprehension to serve the purpose. At any time that we find something important, we may stop and read carefully. After a time we may change back and read rapidly ahead again. This is what is called "a change of pace" in reading.

A change of pace is already familiar to both students and teachers in the handling of content textbooks. The directions for study for such books are usually to read rapidly to get the general impression or situation and then to go back and read carefully to find the answers to certain questions. Here the two types of reading are used one right after the other. English teachers have long used the same system with classics, first telling a class to read the classic rapidly "for the story," and then taking up discussion of problems that require thoughtful reading, section by section.

People who object to permitting children to "read carelessly" or who say that rapid reading produces "bad reading habits'' are simply neglecting this distinction between extensive and intensive reading habits. We must teach both habits, sometimes giving to each habit a separate time, separate method, and separate material, and at other times practicing ''change of pace'' or shifting from one habit to the other.

2. Books must be provided that interest the present type of student and that are at about his reading level.

Extensive reading requires a quantity of books, since children who are reading at their extensive reading speed can cover and should be expected to cover a great deal of ground. These books need to be interesting or the reading will be half-hearted and will produce an antagonism to reading rather than an interest in reading. High school freshman have a wide range of maturity and therefore a wide range of interest. The immature children will require tales of adventure, with rapid moving plot. At the other end of the range, the more mature children will be interested in character studies and social problem books. For the poor readers, it is important to have enough of the simple materials. For some reason there has been an unwillingness to include adventure stories in school libraries. But the immature taste is at the adventure story level, and only such stories will get attentive and eager reading. There are good adventure stories as well as poor ones. Stevenson and Conan Doyle wrote adventure stories.

Students will benefit little from reading if that reading is laborious. Some books must be easy enough for even the poor readers to hurry along and to read with ever increasing interest. The high school reading list must therefore include some books which are as low as fourth grade in reading difficulty. But there must be books suitable for good readers as well. There should also be books as high as twelfth grade reading difficulty, for the purpose is, *"Every* child reading with *interest* at his *present* reading level."

3. Rapid easy reading improves both reading ability and reading taste.

It has often been thought that the children will not learn anything if they read easy material. Experience is sufficient proof that this is not true. The great bulk of reading by all who are now good readers was done on stories and articles which were to them just as easy as the material which we have mentioned will be for the poorest readers in high school. Rapid easy reading improves reading ability because two very definite benefits accrue from it. First, *the recognition of common words is speeded up.* The slow reader takes much time to recognize those simple words which, in constant repetition, make up the bulk of all reading matter. His whole reading process is thus delayed. Those common words appear often in the easy material we recommend. In rapidly reading easy stories, the poor reader is therefore acquiring a skill which will be of much help in all reading. The second benefit of easy reading matter is *enlargement of meaning vocabulary.* No matter how "popular" a story or article may be it is bound to contain some words which are new to the immature reader. Any one who doubts this can easily satisfy himself by handing a simple book to a poor reader and asking him to point out any words he does not know. An adult will be astonished to see how many such words there are. Therefore, easy reading matter will be found steadily but surely to enlarge the child's vocabulary, and the more reading the more enlarging. When the child comes to harder material, this enlarged vocabulary will be very valuable.

It must also be remembered that only easy reading matter can *improve eye movement habits*. Good eye movements are steady, regular, rhythmic steps across the page. These rhythmic steps cannot be taken unless the reading matter is easy, for unknown words and strange ideas immediately break up the progress of the eye movements. Therefore the poor reader can never develop good eye movement habits so long as he is continually presented with hard material. He must be given easy material instead. And there must be a great deal of this easy material. Eye movement habits are like any other habits; they take much practice and repetition for their formation. Smooth, easy, efficient eye movements are not developed from reading a few selections or even a few books. Only many books, read over a long period of time will develop such eye movements. Here is another important reason why there must be *much, rapid, easy* reading for the poor reader.

Not only increased reading ability but also *improved reading tastes* is very likely to result from quantity of reading. Practically all adults who now desire only the best of reading matter will recall that in the beginning of their reading experience, they passed through many stages in the development of their taste. In the very beginning they may not have read only the best books. They may have read much that they now would call trashy. But what is called "trashy" by mature adults is not trashy to children. They see the excitement of rapidly moving plot and they do not see distortion of human nature or of life. The immature mind reads chiefly for plot or action and will always do so. With a growth in maturity of mind, the reader begins to look more critically at the happenings and at the characters. He begins to compare the life and people in the stories with the life and the people about him. The stories begin to appear unreal and foolish. But he still wants to read stories. So he looks for better stories, with more probable happenings and more genuine people. If this process continues long enough, the reader will come to appreciate and desire the best books in the language. But this maturing of mind is a gradual process. It results partly from more years of living. It also results from much reading, for reading is also experience.

In the case of the English teacher herself, this growth in maturity and taste took place very early and very rapidly. We cannot expect such early and rapid development with all children. In fact, with some it is sadly slow and late. With some it may never come. But all experience shows that "much reading leads to better reading." "No reading" obviously leads to nothing.

4. Extensive reading must be made easy and convenient.

In the past, children have been given a reading list, told to get a book from the library, and to go home and read it. Under this system, a minimum of reading has often been done. At present, we plan to secure a great deal of reading by every child, without exception. In fact, the poorer the reader the more reading we wish to secure. Two methods are used to get this result. One is to bring the books as close as possible to the student. The best method is to have the books right in the English room as the room library. The books are furnished by the school library, by the public library, or secured from special funds assigned or collected for the purpose. By this plan the teacher can make sure that each child gets a book and that he gets the right book. A student librarian can attend to the issuing and receiving. Where this plan is not followed, the building librarian can coöperate in getting the right book to the right child.

The second method is to provide for extensive reading on school time. Sometimes one class meeting a week is devoted to rapid reading, sometimes part of a number of class meetings, and sometimes as much as one period a day throughout the week. The rapid reading period may be carried on in the library if conditions permit. It can also be carried on in the classroom if the books are made available. Sometimes a library truckload of books is brought in for an hour and then moved on to another classroom. The teacher is not idle during this rapid reading period, for she circulates among the students, advising, questioning, and otherwise guiding their reading. This rapid reading in school can be considered laboratory experience on a par with laboratory experience in science, art or shop work. It is project work under guidance and direction. It is more profitable than other laboratory work on one score at least. The children are busy all during the rapid reading period and then they are quite likely to take a book home to finish it. In fact, the reading on school time is the best guarantee of reading outside of school time. All schools that have tried this plan report enthusiastically on its success.

5. The widely differing interests of a class must be provided for.

To secure quantity of reading, it is not enough merely to provide easy books. They must appeal to the interests of the children. Those of the girls may be for tales of college, love, marriage, professional success. Those of the boys may be for adventure, exploration, aviation, mechanics, or what not. Adults read eagerly only when they have a book that especially interests them. We cannot expect children to do differently. Fortunately there is an ever increasing flood of books on all subjects that may also interest children. The American Library Association, Chicago, will send book lists and a catalog showing helpful publications. The National Council of Teachers of English, Chicago, has useful lists. The headquarters of the Boy Scouts of America and the Girl Scouts, too, will furnish book lists. *But for poor readers in high school, books should be selected from the grade school lists.* For these children the books must be *easy* as well as interesting.

6. Magazines can be used in the extensive reading plan.

We all know the juvenile magazines, *The American Boy* and *The American Girl, Boy's Life* and the others we see on the newsstands. There are also a number of magazines prepared especially for high school students, such as *The Scholastic, Junior Scholastic, Young America, The American Observer*, etc. Most of these are far simpler reading than the usual high school classics. Poor readers may be greatly helped if the English classroom or the library is supplied with a number of copies of several or all of these magazines. The students will find more pleasure in reading them because they are easier reading. Poor students will be encouraged to put forth more effort because of the interest in stories and timely articles.

Standard magazines for adults also give good reading practice to high school students. The Readers Digest is making a great appeal. It is strange that high school English has so greatly neglected the magazines, which form so large a part of the reading of the American public. Many of our students come from homes that have no magazines at all. They respond quickly and surprisingly to the appeal of the standard magazines. Poor readers find themselves more at home here than with most books. Reading is speeded up and vocabulary is enlarged. Remedial reading can lean heavily on magazines for material.

7. Extensive reading can lead to oral and written English.

Usually, any checkup upon extensive reading is unnecessary, if that reading is done on school time. The teacher can see what is going on. A record of titles, pages and dates can be kept to show the amount read. Sometimes, the record card can bear a simple comment as to whether the book was liked or not, and as to how hard reading it proved. These comments may be studied by the teacher as an aid to better guidance of the child. A student may be permitted to change from one book to another, and in that case, he should record how much of each book he has read. Even if the reading is done outside, no formal checkup is necessary or desirable. The child should not feel he is being watched or his honesty suspected. The teacher who knows the child can tell pretty well how reliable his reports are.

However, quite apart from the keeping of records, it is very desirable that some reaction to every book be encouraged. The child should become accustomed to the question, "Well, what do you think about that book?" The teacher may ask such a question privately at times. Another method is to have each pupil tell the class about any book he found worth while, with the idea of encouraging them to read it too. This is sometimes called "giving a sales talk on the book." Or a pupil may tell a class something interesting he learned from a book. Thus, oral English is encouraged in a natural setting, and both spontaneity and thinking stimulated. Occasionally writing may follow. In this work, each child will be working at his own level and doing his best. The poorest reader can be busily learning how to read and to think without holding back any other child and without being silenced by other children.

8. New emphasis on reading in the regular English course demands that other work be lightened.

Some schools attempt to add emphasis on improving reading to the already greatly overcrowded schedule of work of the English teacher. This creates an impossible situation and little good can be expected. If the English teacher is to emphasize the work we have outlined above, a considerable amount of the work usually put in the freshman course of study must be deferred. There should also be some decision as to how much time shall be given to reading and how much to English.

One solution is to assign definite days to definite topics. One such plan is: Monday, rapid reading; Tuesday, oral or written composition; Wednesday, usage and grammar; Thursday, word study and spelling; Friday, literature.

Different assortments of topics are common and many arrangements are possible to suit different situations; but the principle is the same; the assignment of separate days tends to protect each subject from encroachment by the other. In addition, some teachers think that the change from day to day furnishes a variety which helps maintain the children's interest.

The English course may be planned as a series of "units," each of a certain number of weeks in length. One or more of these may be devoted to remedial reading or to one or more aspects of remedial work. This is a feasible plan when some very definite work is contemplated such as the teaching of syllabication and sounding, or the explaining of some special study skill such as outlining. If, however, some general ability, such as thoughtful reading, needs to be improved, a short period devoted to it can, of course, have little effect. Work throughout a year or more is necessary to get results. Yet the plan of introducing a remedial reading unit or two in the English course does insure a certain amount of time to the subject and is helpful until some more adequate plan is available.

III. Poor readers are sometimes put into separate classes.

A. Large High Schools may have remedial sections of Freshman English.

Some high school English departments divide the Freshman class into sections, either on general ability or on reading ability. Remedial reading work is then supposed to be done in the lowest section since it contains the poor readers. Such sectioning, if thought desirable, had best be done on the basis of the grade teacher's recommendation or on tests given in the grades in May. For the high school to accept children as equal, and then to give them a test and segregate them, is bound to draw attention to the matter and produce ill feeling. Immediate assignment to special sections avoids most of this difficulty.

Some schools feel that a "low" section doing remedial reading is not entitled to regular English credit. The children in it are required to take the regular course either at the same time or later. Other schools call the work regular English and say nothing more about it, only the teacher being supposed to know that it is of special character. In any event, there should be no announcement that children in a low section cannot get a high final grade. Such a policy destroys interest and effort. The case for or against ability sectioning is far too complicated for us to argue it at length here. Whatever its merits, the opinion of the public seems definitely against it. Many of the same advantages can be secured without causing the trouble that ability grouping often brings.

B. Temporary remedial reading groups may be made.

Reading tests can be given to high school students and those who are too badly deficient can be placed in groups for special remedial work. This work is extra work beyond the regular schedule of classes, and the assumption is that each pupil will be excused from it as soon as he has come up to a certain standard. The class may be called "a reading hospital" to which a child is assigned because he needs help and from which he is excused or dismissed as soon as possible. These special groups may be for general reading work or may be for some special type of work in reading. For instance, those scoring too low on a vocabulary test might be assigned to a special group for vocabulary study. Those who cannot pronounce new words might be put into a special group for phonic study. Others who are deficient in some study skill might work upon that skill only. The advantage of this idea is that there is concentration upon one thing at a time and the greatest possible motivation because of the prospect of release as soon as a definite task is accomplished. It also allows a shifting of the group because different children will be deficient in different things.

The drawback to this special group system is that it is an extra load on those who are least able to carry it. Children who can hardly do their regular work are asked to do it and more. It is also likely to be taken as a sort of punishment and resented accordingly. Finally, it assumes that certain very basic disabilities can be removed in a short time. No special class can hope to remove quickly a handicap that is the result of many years of neglect. However, these remedial groups have been found in some cases to increase reading ability on an average of a year in four months time. They are an accepted method of attacking the problem in high school. They tend to be a method for an intensive campaign rather than for a longtime program.[1]

IV. Remedial work in groups is necessarily less effective than individual remedial work.

A. Much less progress is made.

Remedial work in groups has been found to yield averages of twice normal progress. Individual work is generally

---

[1] See *Remedial Reading*, by Monroe and Backus (Houghton Mifflin & Co., 1937), for description of their use in the Washington schools.

found to yield much greater progress than this. In addition, in remedial groups there are often cases that make no progress at all. This is seldom true of individual cases. The reason for this difference is not far to seek. A child improves by the work he himself does. In individual work, the child is working all the time, for the tasks are suited to his needs and the teacher secures his full attention. In a group, the tasks are not always suited to the needs of all the children, for their needs differ more or less. Then each child cannot always be working. Often the members of the class have to take turns. Finally, the teacher cannot secure the full attention of each child all the time. Thus in any half hour of group work, while some of the children may do a full half hour's work, some may do little if any work.

Those planning remedial work must consider advantages and disadvantages of both group and individual work. The usual plan is group work for a large number of children having difficulty and then individual work for the few who do not profit by the group work. The teacher of the group can quickly tell which ones are not benefiting and therefore need the pressure and help of individual attention. At times a few will be found to be so far behind that they cannot fit into any group; they therefore must have individual help if they are to be helped at all. In some schools, the plan is tried of securing a remedial teacher for individual work only. She cannot handle many children at any one time but she rapidly gets some children on their feet and then takes others in their stead.

B. The most effective methods are not yet known.

Most remedial work in reading has been done in clinics or otherwise done individually. Our known methods are chiefly those for individual remedial work. While there has been some group work, it has not been sufficiently studied. We do not have records of just what has been done and just how effective it has been. Thus the teacher who is assigned a remedial group is trying to adapt to a number that which has been developed for use with one. Or she is using standard class room techniques which were not designed for remedial work at all. Here we may have one explanation why group remedial work has not given the results that individual work has secured. We may be able to get much greater results if we could develop more successful group methods. It is to be hoped that scientific studies will be made of this problem. One thing, however, we can be sure of; a library period during which each child reads steadily in a book of direct interest to him and which is of difficulty suitable to his present reading level is a practicable device which results in benefit to all.

CHAPTER IX

STUDY SKILLS

I. The teaching of study should follow certain general principles.

Formerly, "to study" meant to memorize, and directions for study merely gave methods of memorizing verbatim. Rote memorizing is now having less and less importance in the schools, and in its place has come logical memorizing and thinking. This type of study can be divided into a number of processes, of which we shall point out the most important. The ones we shall discuss have general application to many school subjects. There are of course very many others that are applicable only or principally to certain particular school subjects. We can of necessity deal only with general methods and only with the chief of these. But before we take up these methods, some guiding principles must be stated. These apply to all teaching of study and therefore to remedial cases as well as others.

A. Teaching of study must be subordinate to teaching of reading.

Ordinary reading is a rapid, fluent process, the eyes going across the page with a habitual stride, and the mind getting enough comprehension to follow the trend of the author's thought. Study is a slow process, the eyes going slowly and often retracting their steps, the mind getting more than would be possible in ordinary reading. If we had to take our choice, which process would we prefer our pupils to develop? Considering the pupil's needs throughout the rest of his life, we must say that reading is more important than study. Everyone uses reading every day, whether on newspapers, magazines, or books.

This reasoning must convince us that we must first of all teach children to read. We must teach a fluent reading habit. After the child is a good reader, he can develop definite study habits and then, at will, switch from one habit to the other. He may read the first part of an article and then study the balance. Or he may start to study an article and decide it is not worth the time, and read the rest. We want the poor reader to be able to do this, but he cannot until he has really learned to read. Therefore, we should bend all efforts towards the teaching of reading and when that is done teach how to study.

The more mature the child, the more possible it is for us to teach both reading and study without too great interference. The older child can change his purpose and more readily change his method. Thus in high school, we can develop fluent reading in the rapid reading hour and develop careful reading in the intensive study in class. But the student should realize the difference between the two habits and consciously shift from one to the other. This will prevent the very common difficulty of trying to "read" all types of books or trying to "study" all types of them.

B. A few skills well learned are worth more than many touched upon.

Much research has been devoted to the subject of study and, as a result, we have long lists of study abilities.[1] Method of study varies both with purpose and with material. When we consider the great variety of purposes in

---

[1] See Yoakum, G. A., *Reading and Study*. Macmillan Co., New York, 1928.

study, and the many kinds of material worked with, we can understand why so many distinctions between kinds of study can be made. There has therefore been much temptation to prepare for the schools, courses which purport to teach large numbers of study skills.

It is a question whether these complicated courses are suitable to the average high school student, but there are two reasons why these courses are especially inappropriate in classes for poor readers. First, the students in these classes are not ready for a complete course in study. They are slow, immature, discouraged. They can attack only a simple program that appeals to them as immediately practical. Second, there is time for thorough teaching of only a few fundamental skills.

It has been a characteristic of the school barely to touch upon a matter and then to go on to something else. This method is justifiable at times but not when we would teach a skill that is intended to be used. In such a case, there should be thorough teaching. Teaching to study cannot be learned in a few weeks or by a few exercises. Dozens of exercises are necessary. Years may be required. This situation must be seriously considered in any plan to teach study.

C. Study should be taught with study books, not with reading books.

A great mistake of the school has been to select literary material which should be read for enjoyment and then to work on it with study methods. This has been done a great deal by English teachers and has had some most unfortunate results. First, it has given children the idea that a ''good book'' is something to be dissected and analyzed, but never something to be ''read.'' Second, it has failed to teach study very effectively. Literary material was never intended to be used for the teaching of study and is seldom built so as to be the best material for purposes of study. It is not always logically constructed. It seldom shows its outline. And it aims at effect rather than presentation of a factual message.

The best materials for teaching children how to study are the textbooks in their content subjects. This applies to teaching study to all children in high school, not alone to children regarded as remedial cases. Let the children bring their history books to the class in "how-to-study" and teach them how to study a lesson in history. Let them bring their science books and develop the suitable study skills by working on a real lesson. This method of teaching of study impresses the children as being practical and worth while. It solves the problem of where to find study material. It pleases the content teacher who is likely to say that English teachers should teach children how to study. It may even lead to the teaching of study in the content classes according to the principle that "every teacher is a reading teacher," that is, a study teacher.

If content textbooks are not used to teach study, other methods are possible. Four types of material may be used. (1) Books of selections especially planned for teaching study are now issued by many publishers. Some of these books are subject to the criticism that they attempt to teach too many skills and that they do not give enough practice on any single skill to make it usable. Most of them are planned to teach study to the normal high school student rather than to the poor reader. They are too hard for remedial children. (2) The new books of easy reading selections for poor readers are not primarily intended to teach study but they often contain questions which enable teachers to turn them into study books. These questions are really intended as guides for a free and voluntary discussion rather than as exercises to be done, but they can be used as exercises if the chief emphasis is kept upon the interest of the reading matter. (3) The books of literary selections which are often used in high school English often have work books which go along with them. These may be used to teach study but they violate the principle stated above that reading materials that should be read for pleasure should not be subjected to the same kind of study that is used in the sciences. If the literature work books are truly suited to the teaching of literature as literature they will not be the best for the teaching of study.

Perhaps the most successful study books are the various exercise books that have been published for this purpose. They have many short selections upon which questions are asked. They therefore emphasize strongly the word, sentence and paragraph, just the emphasis needed by poor readers rather than the analysis of a long selection that is more appropriate for skilled readers. Of the various exercise books, perhaps the Standard Test Lessons in Reading[2]

---

[2] *Standard Test Lessons in Reading,* McCall-Crabbe, Bureau of Publications, Teachers College, New York City, are issued in a wide range of difficulty. Be sure to use one that is fully easy enough. *The Experiments in Reading,* McCall, Nowell, and Cook (also Bureau of Publications, Teachers College), are intended for normal high school students and are therefore not easy enough for remedial pupils. The Practice Exercises in Reading, Gates-Peardon (also Bureau of Publications, Teachers College), are issued in different degrees of difficulty but have the objection that they train only in the four types of reading represented by the Gates Silent Reading Test and are therefore not as broad a taining as the Standard Test Lessons.

have been found most valuable in remedial work. Most of the material, especially in the upper books, is study material and not literary material. Because there are different books at various reading levels, a book can be chosen which is easy enough for the particular class in mind. Study skills are best developed when the material is of only moderate difficulty. Study of these daily lessons becomes an interesting game because each lesson is scored and each child can try to beat his own record. Because no marks are made in the books and they can therefore be used over and over again, they are inexpensive.

II. A few definite study skills can be successfully taught.

As already suggested, it is better to concentrate on a few skills or habits and teach them well than to scatter effort over a good many. We therefore discuss below the skills that need to be attacked first and that can be most successfully taught.

A. Skill in use of the dictionary is important in most study.

Study materials are hard. They contain new words. They cannot be fully understood unless the meaning of those words is discovered. Hence, the dictionary. There are now many books or pamphlets on the use of the dictionary, one of which every teacher should possess. Some of them may be secured free by writing to dictionary publishers. There are also books on how to teach the use of the dictionary. But the best way for a child to learn to use a dictionary is to have much practice in its actual use. In any room in which study is being taught, there should be a dictionary on each pupil's desk. When a strange word is met with, the dictionary should be opened up and used. It should become a familiar tool. Yet the dictionary should be used in the spirit of fun, to satisfy curiosity, and to find interesting things about words. If children dislike the dictionary, it will never be used outside of class no matter how many lessons are given on it. The pupil's usual method with strange words is to guess at the meaning or to skip the word and go on. And that method will continue to be used unless children find the dictionary an interesting book. This is one of the best arguments for use of one of the new, attractive dictionaries with definitions especially written to be understood by children.

The skills used in finding a word in the dictionary and in figuring out the pronunciation are taught first but these are only preliminary to the finding of meaning, which is the real value of the dictionary for study. Study requires the finding out of meaning. As the dictionary shows, most words have various or many meanings. The real skill consists in telling which meaning belongs in the sentence we are considering. This is the problem to be emphasized when a class looks up a word found in study material. The usual test for selection of the proper meaning is whether it fits into the context. Children who do not apply this test often get ridiculous results when they try to locate the meaning of a word in the dictionary. The teacher can bring this point home by having every meaning that is given used in the context so as to show that only one of them fits in. This should be done several times to impress on the children that they do not want *a* meaning of the word but only the *right* meaning.

B. Finding answers to fact questions is a widely useful study skill.

Study is reading with a purpose, and the usual purpose which the teacher gives the pupil is to find the answer to a fact question. We may ask a child to read hurriedly over something to get a general conception of it, but the study begins when he comes to the questions and starts going over the material again in order to find the answers. He knows that somewhere in the reading matter is a word or phrase or statement which gives the answer he wants. How shall he find it?

The method of this kind of study may be described as rapid reading, or skimming, with some particular cue in mind. If we are looking for some fact about a person, we skim rapidly, looking for his name. If we want to know what happened at a certain date, we skim rapidly looking for the particular figures. Any fact we may want to locate has some word cue that we may look for. Of course, we do not look just anywhere, but figure out in what part of the material the fact is likely to be. As soon as we find the cue or some other cue that may seem connected with our purpose, we instantly slow down and read slowly and thoughtfully. When we locate the fact, we look carefully at it, read it over and over, underline it or copy it out. Thus we have a general description of the method of study for the answer to a fact question. Much practice develops great skill and rapidity in the process.

C. The most useful study skill is finding answers to thought questions.

As we have said, study is reading with a purpose. One purpose, the finding an answer to a fact question, we have just discussed. A more important purpose is finding the answer to a thought question. When the pupil knows what fact he is looking for, his problem of study is relatively simple. But in answering thought questions he does not know just what facts he needs. He knows only the problem that is to be solved. He must find anything or everything which may be useful.

Fact questions and thought questions are easily confused. The question, "Why did the French, who explored the Middle West, fail to hold it?" sounds like a thought question. It may or may not be. If the question means "What reason do the books give to explain why the French did not hold the Middle West?" then we have a fact question. If the question means, "Do you, after considering all the facts come to a conclusion of your own or agree with the reason the books give?" then we have a thought question instead. Study to answer a thought question includes the finding of facts, but does not tell beforehand just what facts to find. It also includes comparing and evaluating facts and coming to a personal conclusion. It is the most important type of study a school can teach, and it can be taught only by practice. Not nearly enough time is now given to this type of study.

The study technique in this case is similar to that described for the finding of answers to fact questions, but it is more difficult. Because a thought question is more general than a fact question, there is more uncertainty as to where to look for material. One asks himself, "Where would I be likely to find something bearing on the question?" The second step is rapid reading or skimming, but not, in this case, with one particular cue in mind. Instead, one is looking for anything related to his question. The whole problem must be kept in mind, and many cues may lead to the desired material. The reading is therefore slower and more thoughtful. When something that seems useful is found, it is read carefully and evaluated. If it seems valuable, a note is made, and the reading goes on. The answer is usually not found at one place but instead many facts have to be gathered. The final step is deciding when the gradually accumulated information gives the answer desired.

D. We may aid study by teaching methods of reference reading.

The types of study we have mentioned should imply the wide use of books. Such use implies two types of skill. First, we have methods of *locating materials that we wish to read.* (1) In a dictionary, for instance, one wishes to read a single definition, but must first locate that definition. (2) In an encyclopaedia, one wishes to read a single article, but must first find that article. (3) In a bound magazine file, one also must find an article to be read. (4) In a book one must locate a chapter or a paragraph. (5) In a library one must know how to locate a single book. In all these cases there are definite techniques for locating material to be read. This may be made a fascinating subject for children. It involves a sort of hide and seek, a type of detective work. A teacher who does not understand fully methods of locating materials should have a conference with a reference librarian. Books on the use of libraries also give much valuable information.[3] A trip to a library, which

---

[3] A useful and interesting book is the *Child's Guide to the Use of Libraries,* by Mott and Boisder, Chas. Scribners Sons. New York.

includes explanation and demonstration of all its resources, is fascinating to children at every level. In fact, methods of locating information to be read are indispensable to any really intelligent study.

A second skill, *skimming*, is required for wide use of books. It is often used after one has located the information to be read. Suppose the pupil, looking for information, finds in the encyclopaedia the article on Venetian glass. He may not wish to find all about Venetian glass but only certain facts about it.[4] For instance, he may wish to know how long ago Venetian glass was first made (fact question) or how Venetian glass may have affected glass making today (thought question). In either case, he would not need to read every word in the entire article, but he would skim it instead. One kind of skimming is done by running the eyes over the material faster than it is possible to read. To answer the fact question about Venetian glass, one might run his eyes down the column looking for dates. When a date appeared, the eyes would stop and the sentence would be read to see what the date meant. This kind of skimming is widely used when one is answering fact questions and has a cue such as a name in mind. The eye can move rapidly until it catches the name and stops. The second kind of skimming means *reading selected parts*. In the case of determining the beginning of Venetian glass, one would naturally read the beginning of the article to find the answer. To find material which would suggest the

---

[4] To find out "all about" a subject is a purpose not often given younger students because of the large amount of labor and time involved. It is a type of study that should, however, be used on occasion. It requires slow, careful reading.

influence of Venetian glass on modern glass, one would naturally look at the end of the article. In skimming an article or a chapter of a book by this method one would read the first and last sections to see if the whole chapter were not summarized at these places. Or one may go through a chapter reading just the beginnings of paragraphs to see what the chapter covers. These methods must be taught to children if we expect them to use reference books efficiently. They become important skills through practice and are used constantly by educated people who must look through more books and magazines every month than they can possibly read entire.

E. Outlining is indirect training in study.

The use of outlining is fundamental in writing. Any mass of material to be written up must be presented in some orderly fashion, and it is brought into order by outlining in the author's mind, whether he makes the outline apparent or not. Work poorly outlined may be interesting to read, but the reader will not have a clear conception of the author's thought when he is through, or he may have a quite mistaken conception of it.

It has long been the custom to teach outlining as a method of study. We should therefore connect outlining with the two study skills that we have pointed out, finding the answer to a fact question, and finding the answer to a thought question. When one has made an outline of an author's work, in what type of study has he then been engaged? Obviously, he has answered the thought question, "What is the author's message?" The process has been one of "reading with a problem in mind." There may also have been very definite fact-study in searching for cues such as the verbal signs of structure, "first," "then," "finally," "another," and the like, but there were also the more general questions, "What are the important points?", "What does this paragraph deal with?" and the like. Therefore we may say that outlining is a process that combines the two processes of fact study and thought study.

Yet outlining as a study technique should not be placed before these two other types of study. First, the problem in outlining, "What is the author's message?" is a problem that appears chiefly in school rather than outside. In after life one does not often outline an author's message. He does so only when he wants to repeat it to someone else. In the case of most reading, the reader is looking for a certain fact or for the solution of some problem of his own. He therefore uses the author's work in his own way, and does not seek a complete picture of the author's message. Second, if practice in logical thinking is desired it is better for a student to gather material and organize it than merely to go over a lot that has already been organized and set down by someone else. Outlining author's thoughts should be only a preliminary step to outlining one's own thoughts. Therefore we may conclude that outlining is good practice in thinking, that it is useful in locating what authors have to say, and that it furnishes a model for the organizing of the students own material. But the teaching of outlining should not keep us from teaching the better type of thought study, which is the defining of problems, the finding of materials that might help solve them, and the evaluating and organizing of that material.

CHAPTER X

TESTING AND REMEDIAL READING

I. Some general principles are to be observed in all testing.

We shall deal in this chapter with testing only as it concerns remedial reading. The teacher is undoubtedly already familiar with educational measurements and may have given many tests herself. The more experience she has had with tests the better, because one learns about tests through using them.

There is much divergent opinion among teachers about the use of tests; yet tests are absolutely essential in one form or another in remedial work. We shall therefore treat the matter as simply and as objectively as possible, basing all statements upon results from actual use of tests with remedial cases in reading.

A. Do not scare the child with tests.

A much too common procedure is to bring a child into a strange room, confront him with a strange person, and give him a whole series of strange, hard tasks, which we call tests. This is scarcely humane, to begin with; second, it is not likely to get the most accurate results; and third, it does not form a good start for such a difficult process as remedial reading. Finally, it is not necessary. It is true that many tests may be given at once at a Reading Clinic where it is desired to get the greatest amount of objective data in the least possible time but even in the clinic great care is taken first to make friends with the child and put him at his ease.

In the public school, cases for remedial reading are easily selected as a result of their school records and the reports of teachers who have had them previously (see Appendix A for a Teacher's Report Form). If, then, we know that a child is a poor reader, we do not need to begin with tests, but should begin in the natural way by making friends. We talk to him, interest him in some way, find out his likes and dislikes. Soon we will have him read something that we are sure he can read and that he will like. Then gradually we will give tests. These will, in effect, be games to give variety to the lesson. They may extend over several weeks. We might like to know all the child's abilities on a certain day, but we want the benefits to the child to take preference over any statistical recording of results. For both these reasons, we introduce testing gradually. This principle applies also when group work is undertaken.

B. Tests are to aid the teacher's judgment, not to replace it.

We have repeatedly pointed out that each case in remedial reading is a unique combination of difficulties and causes and that the teacher is the professional expert who brings to bear upon each individual case her store of experience with children and with reading. She studies the individual and comes to a conclusion as to the sort of reading he does, its good points and its bad points, and what deficiencies may or may not be corrected. The teacher uses reading tests to aid her in this study of the individual, but she uses these tests wisely and not blindly. She gives various tests, some similar to one another and some different. She tries the new tests as they come out. She experiments with tests. Yet she realizes that it is her place to make the final analysis of a child's reading and to pass judgment upon it. The reading tests aid her but cannot take the place of her mature judgment.

C. Check one test against another.

No teacher will place full reliance upon a single test. All tests make mistakes. These mistakes may be rare, but the trouble is we cannot tell which case is the mistake and which is not. Suppose there is only one mistake in a hundred cases; is this case before us the one mistake or not?

Then, even under the best of conditions, a test score is only an approximation. Children taking tests do better at one time than another. They may do poorly for all sorts of reasons. Therefore, the only safe course is to give at least several tests and compare the results. Two tests which agree reassure that we are getting at the facts. If three tests agree, we become confident indeed. However, tests of different type must not be expected to agree completely. They may be testing somewhat different combination of abilities. Only by much experience with many kinds of tests can one learn when to expect test scores to come out the same and how to interpret their differences.

II. Intelligence tests are essential.

We must know how much intelligence poor readers have because we must know how much ability they have to work with. We are all inclined to judge intelligence of children by their appearance and their actions. For instance, children usually play with other children of their own mental age, so that playing with younger children suggests mental backwardness. Yet it is easy to be deceived in these matters. Children who are lively in manner and sociable are usually thought to be brighter than they really are. Children who have been given extra promotion will be young for their group and will be thought by the teacher to be less intelligent than they really are.

For all these reasons it is essential to give intelligence tests to poor readers. Very often a child who is reading a year or two behind the rest of his class will be found to have a mental age that is a year or two behind theirs. He may thus be reading up to his real ability and not actually be retarded at all. However, the usual situation is for a child's retardation in reading to be greater than his backwardness in intelligence. That is, a child one year behind the mental age for his grade is likely to be two years or more behind in reading ability. One reason for this is probably that low intelligence carries with it other handicaps, or makes all other handicaps worse. Another is that most reading materials and instruction have been ill adapted to slow learners and therefore they have not been able to progress even as well as they might.

An especial reason for giving intelligence tests is that we are prone to jump to the conclusion the poor readers are mentally dull. We reason that a child of normal intelligence would be bound to learn to read as normal children do. But when an intelligence test shows normal or nearly normal intelligence, or sometimes more than normal, we are forced to believe that special attention is necessary since, in spite of adequate ability, the usual methods have failed to take effect.

A. Use non-verbal tests on non-readers or poor readers.

Any intelligence test which requires reading is unsuited for use with poor readers. The usual recourse is to the Binet Individual Intelligence Test. This test is difficult to give both because equipment is necessary and because it should be given by an experienced person. In its stead it is now possible to use the Chicago Non-verbal Examination.

(Institute of Juvenile Research, Chicago, Illinois.) This test contains no reading whatever and seems to give very usable results. It is also possible to use the first part of the Kuhlman-Anderson test, which is also non-verbal. (Educational Test Bureau, Minneapolis, Minn.) The nonverbal parts will measure mental ages up to about ten years. If possible, both these tests should be given so that the results may be checked one against the other. These tests, like any others, should be used only after the remedial teacher has secured the child's full confidence. They should be administered as games, where one does his best but does not worry about the result.

B. Remember that there are different kinds of intelligence.

Some persons are thrown completely out of sympathy with a child as soon as they find he makes a low score on an intelligence test. But we should remember that the tests usually measure what might be called academic intelligence, or the kind required for success in the ordinary school. The child who scores low on this ability may still make a success in life. There are other kinds of ability than academic intelligence. For instance, mechanical intelligence is needed for many vocations and social intelligence for many others. These and other types of ability may be present when "school ability" is limited.

Another thing to remember is that character qualities are necessary to make a successful and useful citizen. The adult world needs persons with industry and perseverance. It requires loyalty and reliability. It rewards those who have cheerfulness and friendliness. This is a fact which must be considered when we find a child making a low score on an intelligence test. Intelligence is not the only factor to consider. We must keep all these things in mind when dealing with the children who, because they are poor readers, come to our unfavorable attention in school. And we must seek to develop all these good character qualities and not their opposites.

C. Do not be over-influenced or under-influenced by test results.

People tend to go to extremes with regard to intelligence tests. They either accept a result with perfect faith or they discount the test altogether. A middle ground is the proper one. After experience with intelligence tests, one comes to realize that the results are of very positive value. If the test is properly given, a low score shows that something is certainly wrong. Experience makes one rather cautious, however, in deciding just what is wrong. Is the difficulty emotional so that ability did not have a chance to show itself? Are only certain abilities low while other may be normal or better? Is there low ability in everything? Deficiencies may even be in habits of attention rather than in native ability, after all. When one knows a child very well and then gives him intelligence tests, these questions are bound to arise in the mind. That is why we must say that intelligence tests results should be used wisely and in the light of everything else that one knows about a child. One must be careful not to be over-influenced or under-influenced by results.

III. Reading tests must be used with understanding.

A. A reading test limits material read, limits time of reading, and limits the child's response.

The teacher can understand the place of reading tests better if she will consider what a reading test is. It is essentially a short piece of reading matter that is to cause a child to make a certain definite response in a certain time. The response is usually marking a certain word. The child who marks the right word in the given time is assumed to have the kind of reading ability that average children of a certain grade have. The child who does not mark the word in the time given is assumed not to have that average ability. The test tells that in a certain short time the child made the same mark that the other children made or that he did not make that same mark.

The teacher will see at once certain problems in this testing procedure. *First*, the child is given only a short piece to read. The teacher who is testing a child might have him read quite a long story. Can we tell enough about a child's reading from the short piece given by the test? *Second*, the reading test strictly limits the time. Does this great emphasis on speed give the right impression of a child's reading? Practically every reading test is a timed test, but teachers want to know *what* a child can do rather than how *fast* he can do it. Teachers will always be careful when using test scores based on timing because such scores greatly overemphasize the factor of how much a child can do in a limited time. We seldom strictly limit time in this way in school. We give and urge the taking of whatever time is necessary.

Third, the test tells only that the child did or did not mark a certain word or set of words. How much did the child understand? What kind of thinking or reading actually went on? The scores give a very poor answer to these questions. Experience shows that some children follow strange methods in doing reading tests. Some may do a good deal of thinking to find the right word and some may do very little. When a teacher works with a child she may ask many questions. She varies her questions until she is sure she knows how the child reads and how well he reads. The test cannot do this. The test is limited. It is limited in all three of the ways we have mentioned, limited material, limited time, and limited questions. When a teacher is working with an individual child, she is not limited in any of these ways.

B. All tests results need to be checked with actual reading.

Reading tests may be used on a large group to discover "suspects," that is, pupils whom we think to be poor readers. We then take the "suspect" and have him really read. We have him read a good deal of material of different levels and kinds. There is no reason to hurry over the process. The test is an indication, the reading is final proof. As already suggested, a good plan is to have at hand a set of well graded readers, not marked for grades, and test a child's reading by having him read a page or two out of several of them. Different types of questions can then be asked to determine amount of understanding.

C. Too much attention has been paid to grade standards in reading.

If a child does not make the "standard score" for his grade, this does not necessarily mean his reading is unsatisfactory; if he makes the standard score or above this does not necessarily mean his reading *is* satisfactory. Yet such is the too common conclusion of teachers and superintendents using reading tests. The "standard grade score" on any test is the arithmetic average of the scores of many children in all kinds of schools in all parts of the country. Good schools and poor schools, dull children and bright children, all are included. Their scores spread far up and far down. For instance, the fifth grade "standard" is the average of scores ranging from perhaps third grade ability to seventh. Should every fifth grade child in every school then reach this standard or be satisfied if he reaches it?

The fact is that many children and many schools are so handicapped that they should not be expected to reach the "grade standard." Other children and schools should be expected to far exceed the "grade standard." It is of value to know what the grade standard of tests is, but what we expect of any school or any child depends on a knowledge of that school and of that child. "Grade standards" should not cause undue worry or give us a false self-complacency.

D. Older poor readers will grade on most reading tests beyond their real ability.

Every reading test implies two processes. The first is the reading. The second is making the required response. It is this second process that the unreliability with poor readers probably arises. The poor reader, it must be remembered, is a child whose age, and usually whose mental ability, is beyond the grade level of the test. His ability at making the response is therefore greater than his ability in doing the reading. Thus he gets a score which is beyond his true reading level. For instance, a fourth grader who cannot read a primer, will score second grade on many primary reading tests. A fourth grader who can only read second readers may score 4B on a reading test. These children have become expert at guessing from pictures. Or they compare words and get the right answer without having been able to read a sentence. Here is an annoying situation that causes us more than ever to emphasize that the test of reading is reading and that reading tests must be used with understanding.

E. Check guessing by having the tests done over orally.

As we have just suggested, part of the reading test score is reading and part of it may be guessing. It is important to know how much is one and how much the other. This can be determined very easily by first giving the test according to directions and then by having the child read the test aloud. On a second test sheet, the words which he cannot pronounce or mispronounces should be marked as in an oral reading test. Additions and omissions should also be marked. This method quickly shows whether a right answer was due to reading or to guessing. It is an absolutely essential precaution when reading tests are used with poor readers.

F. The reading matter on the test must be of about the child's true reading level.

Any material which is beyond the child's actual reading ability requires a process of puzzling out that is not reading and is not a true measure of reading ability. If a test designed for a certain grade is given to that grade, it is seldom fair or satisfactory for the poor readers. Therefore the first reading test given to a large group to pick out the poor readers must not be regarded as final. The poor readers must be separated and given another reading test which has reading material nearer their true reading level. Reading tests of several levels may be tried with advantage. When the teacher already knows what a child's approximate reading level is, she may pick a test that is suitable.

IV. Certain tests have particular usefulness in remedial reading.

We shall now discuss the use of certain well-known tests, giving advantages and disadvantages as found in practice with remedial reading cases, leaving it to the individual teacher to try out the ones which seem to suit her purpose and make her own final decision.

Again we must emphasize that we are suggesting methods for the classroom teacher and not for the reading clinic. Clinical methods are detailed and refined. Much time is given and methods are possible that are learned only by long practice. The class room teacher must use tests that are more easily applied. She must also be able to interpret results from the type of tests usually purchased by superintendents for survey purposes, and that are not especially planned to be diagnostic.

A. Gray's Oral Reading Paragraphs.

With an individual case, the first test the teacher will use is a copy of Gray's Oral Reading Paragraphs. This is an inexpensive sheet containing fifteen paragraphs, the first of primer difficulty and the others gradually stepping up to what is probably college level. The child is handed one sheet and asked to read aloud. If he is a very poor reader, he starts at the beginning; if not, at any paragraph the teacher may indicate. The teacher has another copy of the test before her and marks upon it, without attracting the pupil's attention, just what he does as he reads. She shows omissions, insertions, mispronouncing, failure to pronounce, and other characteristics of the reading. In each succeeding paragraph, the difficulties and errors will increase until she tells the pupil to stop. The test recommends that seven mistakes in each of two succeeding paragraphs cause the testing to stop, but the teacher will use the test as best suits her own purposes. Sometimes she will let the pupil attack material that is very hard for him just to see what he will do. At other times she will stop him early to avoid discouragement.

The directions for the test tell how it may be used to secure a grade standing in both speed and accuracy. The writer suggests, however, that such grade standing may be secured in other ways and that, instead, this test be used chiefly as an exploratory device. It gives the teacher in a few minutes a general picture of the child's reading situation. Since she is experienced, this will tell her about what grade of material he is ready to read. This is really what she wants to know. At the same time this test is very diagnostic, telling her about his sight vocabulary, his sounding ability, his use of context, and his other reading habits. There is nothing quite as useful as this test in the hands of an experienced teacher, in making a rapid first analysis of a remedial reading case. (Public School Publishing Co., Bloomington, Ill.)

B. The Dolch-Gray Word Recognition Test.

If oral reading paragraphs show that a child has insufficient capital of sight words, we wish to know just what that capital is. A quick test of sight vocabulary can be made with the Dolch-Gray Word Recognition Test. There are three of these sheets, each containing 100 words, or 300 words in all. A child can be given a sheet and asked to read off the words. The teacher can hold another sheet and mark on it what the child does, just as described in case of the Gray Oral Reading Paragraphs, showing refusals, mispronouncing, additions, omissions, etc. (Scott-Foresman & Co., Chicago, Ill.)

Another means is use of the 220 basic sight vocabulary cards described on page 53. The teacher can run the child through these cards in two or three minutes and then have a clear and definite statement of what his sight vocabulary situation is. If he is a very poor reader, she may sort the cards into two or three packs according to difficulty and then begin with the easiest pack so as to avoid discouraging the child at the start. A child who has average third grade reading ability will be found to know practically all of the basic sight words. (The Garrard Press, Champaign, Ill.)

C. The Detroit Reading Test.

The Detroit Reading Test has the great advantage of beginning at the second grade level and having different tests also at the third grade level and the fourth grade level. Thus it enables us to give very poor readers something which is at about their present reading level. This is very important. The test is in two forms so that it may be given before and after training. It is inexpensive. If the test for one grade level is tried and seems too hard or too easy, the test for the level below or above may also be given. In using the test, one should take the precaution of having the child read it orally after he has done it silently. The teacher should mark each word he cannot pronounce. This precaution is advisable because the even items on the test are answered by marking a single word, and some children do this marking simply by finding one of the words in the paragraph. The norms given for this test are not as complete as they should be for remedial reading purposes. (World Book Co., Chicago, Ill.)

D. Gates Reading Survey for Grades 3 to 10.

The Gates Reading Survey is of quite wide usefulness in Remedial Work. It is in three parts (1) Vocabulary, (2) Level of Comprehension, (3) Speed and Accuracy, each part having separate norms so that the child's performance on each can be judged separately. This is very important. Then the tests have wide range. Test 3, to measure Speed and Accuracy, consists of short paragraphs composed of short sentences that can be attempted without discouragement by children who are reading almost as low as second grade. Test 1, Vocabulary, begins with very easy words so that a poor reader can do something on it, though it is necessary to watch him and stop the test when he has reached his limit, to prevent too great a sense of failure. Test 2, Level of Comprehension, is a scale running from easy paragraphs to very hard paragraphs. Remedial cases can make some progress with it but again must not be allowed to become discouraged. Here is another illustration that tests must not be given in a mechanical fashion but instead with a constant watching of the child's reactions. (Bureau of Publications, Teachers College, New York.)

E. The Gates Silent Reading Tests.

The reading matter in the Gates Silent Reading Tests, though intended for grades 3 to 8, is all at one level of difficulty, about grades 4 or 5. Therefore these tests are excellent for use with children whose actual reading ability ranges from fourth grade to sixth grade. Readers at lower reading levels find too many hard words and therefore do too much guessing. High school teachers who have readers as low as fourth to sixth grades can use these tests to advantage. For first testing of a large group only one type needs to be used as this makes the testing quite inexpensive. It is recommended that type D, ''Reading for Details,'' be chosen because it is perhaps closest to the kind of thing these children are supposed to be doing with their high school textbooks. If, however, the teacher is concerned with the child's outside reading she would choose type A, ''Reading to Predict Coming Events.'' For a remedial case, the ''Reading to Follow Directions'' is probably best because one can watch best the child's thought processes. Here is a clear case in which the teacher's purpose influences her choice of tests. For better understanding of the remedial cases, all four of the Gates Tests are helpful. (Bureau of Publications, Teachers College, New York.)

F. The Inglis Vocabulary Test (Grades 6 to 10).

High school teachers will find poor vocabulary an outstanding characteristic of poor readers. They will want to give a test which uses as large a number of words as possible so as to get a good sample of the child's vocabulary. These words should not include easy ones which every one knows or too hard ones which only very good readers would know. Of the various vocabulary tests, the Inglis test perhaps meets best these two requirements. The test is in two forms and has adequate grade standards. (Ginn & Co., Boston, Mass.)

G. The New Stanford and the Metropolitan Achievement tests.

These survey tests have sections upon reading which are widely used from the middle grades on to pick out ''suspects'' for further investigation. They serve this purpose satisfactory. The reading sections are short, however, and measure only one or two aspects of reading. Therefore it is to be understood that pupils scoring low on such general tests as these should be given other tests which will find out more about their difficulties. If other tests are not available, the teacher can have the suspects read to her and thus make a further diagnosis. (World Book Co., Chicago, Ill.)

H. The Iowa Silent Reading Test, for Grades 4 to 9.

Junior and senior high schools have found this test quite suitable for studying poor readers because of the types of material it contains. There is a vocabulary section, divided into "General Vocabulary" and "Subject Matter Vocabulary." There is study reading of typical textbook material in history and science (geography). There is a speed of reading section, and there are tests in alphabetizing, and in the use of index. A section on "Selection of Central Idea" represents one of the more important of the study skills. The types of materials and the types of reading covered by this test fit school needs so well as to make it a very popular test. The teacher may use as much of this test as she thinks suits her purpose. She may study the scores of separate sections rather than use the total score. (World Book Co., Chicago, Ill.)

I. Diagnostic Tests.

The teacher who is interested in analysis of reading difficulties should try out the various sets of diagnostic reading tests. Each of these consists of a series of subtests, each one intended to determine amount of deficiency in a single aspect of reading. Practice in giving these tests is needed if sound results are to be obtained. Three Diagnostic Tests, in order of publication, are the Monroe Diagnostic Reading Test, (C. H. Stoelting Company, Chicago, 1932). The Gates Reading Diagnosis Tests, (Bureau of Publications, Teachers College, Columbia University, New York, 1933). The Durrell Analysis of Reading Difficulties, (World Book Company, New York, 1938).

Even if one does not intend to use these tests, it is very profitable to get a sample set and study them to see what they consider separate aspects of reading difficulty. For instance, the sub-tests of two diagnostic tests are:

GATES

Oral Context-Reading
Graded Word Pronunciation
Tests of Word Recognition Techniques
Visual Perception
Also the following separate tests:
    Word Recognition
    Sentence Reading
    Paragraph Reading (Primary)
    General Impression
    Predicted Outcome
    Directions
    Details

DURRELL

Oral Reading Comprehension
Oral Reading—Unaided Oral Recall
Silent Reading—Unaided Oral Recall
Flashed Word—Word Analysis Test
Phonetic Inventory
Silent Reading—Written Recall
Difficulties in Writing and Spelling
Informal Tests

From a study of these sub-tests, the teacher can better decide what she believes to be the essential aspects of reading difficulty. She can then be on the lookout for those aspects both in her use of other tests and in her listening to children's reading. She may even decide to use some of these sub-tests on certain cases where she suspects a special difficulty. In this way every teacher should try to make use in her own work of the work of the experts who have made these diagnostic tests.

CHAPTER XI

PREVENTION

I. Some remedial reading will always be with us.

The best-laid curriculum plans will always miscarry to some extent. There will never be an adequate supply of the ideal type of teacher. With every possible motivation, we shall never be able to get the full pupil coöperation that would be needed if each child were to reach his maximum achievement. And, finally, there will always be sickness that keeps children out of school, and the moving about of parents that disturbs school attendance. All of these factors will operate to keep school work from being all that it should be. Yet, though we will realize that our efforts will never be entirely successful, we should use all of our knowledge and intelligence in doing everything conceivable to reduce the need for remedial work to its absolute minimum.

A definite step to lessen remedial reading will be to raise the level of all reading instructions. To this end, all teachers should become familiar with the Research Bulletin of the National Education Association, entitled "Better Reading Instruction" which can be obtained for 25c from the National Education Association, Washington, D. C. This survey of the practices of successful teachers of reading is full of excellent practical ideas.

II. Beginning failures can be avoided.

As we have seen, non-readers have two striking characteristics; they dislike reading and they do not believe they can learn to read. These feelings and ideas have their chief source in grade one. All school men now know there is such a thing as reading readiness and that, if we attempt to teach a child to read before he has reading readiness, he is bound to fail. Here is the superintendent's first chance at prevention. He can have a first grade program which develops a child in language, in attention, and in perception up to the point where he is sure to begin reading with success. This program will include activities from the beginning of school that will develop the child socially, give him self-confidence, and result in the making of experience charts that will pave the way to reading. The program may suggest beginning reading with the advanced group in September, with the slower group, perhaps, in December or January, and with the slowest, perhaps not until March or April. The teacher will watch for reading readiness, which is essentially the ability to identify individual words, or she may use reading readiness tests. It is not so much a question whether this slower group are or are not retained in grade one. Many factors, such as even the number of seats, will influence that matter. The important thing is that when each child finally starts to read, he should find it a successful, meaningful, and happy experience. One factor in this success for all is careful physical examination and correction of sensory defects.

Far too often, the school has required that first grade teachers follow a certain prescribed program or schedule for all children, and they have done so at great cost in discouragement and failure. Instead, first grade teachers should work with each group of children in the way that group requires. We need never fear that learning to read will be unnecessarily delayed. Even if children start a little later than they might have started, they will rapidly catch up if they like reading, for they immediately of their own accord put extra time and effort on the subject. Here in the proper beginning of reading we have the first essential step for prevention of the tremendous drag of remedial reading throughout the school system.

III. Children must be given books that they can read.

Superintendents, school boards, and patrons seem possessed of the notion that school is a series of stair steps and that each step demands a new set of books a step harder in difficulty. The child is pushed on to harder and harder jobs with the assumption that if the teacher brings enough pressure to bear, the child will somehow be able to do them. The proper learning is supposed to result.

The superintendents and the business men on the board who have this conception of the school need to have one fact called to their attention. It is true that they assign jobs to their employees and the employees must do them. But they must remember that if the individual cannot do the job, they "fire" him. It is upon the principle of throwing out the incompetent that the whole system of "making people do a job" is based. But just let the business man or the superintendent imagine a quite different situation. Let him assume the situation that he could fire nobody. Then we would have only one recourse: If the people could not do the job, he would have to make the job easier. That is the situation in the school. The children cannot be put out. They cannot be "fired." If they cannot do a job, the job has to be made easier.

Now it is a fact attested by all who have studied the matter carefully that about one-third of the children in grade school are supplied every year with books that they

cannot read. Struggling with those books, they increase
their reading ability little if any. What they do do is to
increase their dislike for reading, and they therefore do
everything in their power to avoid all reading. If they are
poor readers this year, they are relatively worse readers
next year when moved on to the next grade. Each year they
make less than a year's progress and therefore trail further
and further behind the others. Keeping the poor readers
two years in one room does not solve the difficulty if the
books are still too hard and if the child still does not want
to learn. Only books within their ability and a motive
for using them will cause them to begin to improve.

**A. Adoption of easy texts is a partial solution of the
reading problem.**

There is nowadays an evergrowing demand for textbooks
in all fields that are easier to read. Publishing companies
are rising to the occasion and are revising old books or
issuing new books which have simpler reading matter. As
soon as an easier book is adopted, many children become
satisfactory readers who were classed as unsatisfactory
before. Children who were serious remedial cases become
less serious. Children who were learning little or nothing
take new interest and begin to improve. The whole atmos-
phere of a room may be changed by an easier textbook.
This solution is partial, but it has such a sweeping effect
that it deserves speedy adoption. It involves no change in
administrative methods, and arouses only favorable comments from parents. The adoption of easier texts is an easy
and direct method of lessening remedial reading. We must
emphasize, however, that this method has a definite limit.

As soon as the books are truly suited to a grade, no further change is desirable.

B. Supplying different sections with different sets of books should be the rule in each of the primary grades.

Because some children start to read later than others, the primary rooms will each contain a wide range of reading ability. First graders will range from non-readers to second grade readers. The second grade room will have from primer readers to third grade readers. The third grade will have from first grade readers to fourth or fifth grade readers. This fact must be recognized by suitable grouping in each grade and by giving to each group a book that is at its level. Each primary room therefore needs at least three different sets of readers representing three different levels. The recently published textbooks are given names and are not marked with a grade so that books of three different grade levels can be used in one room without comment by children or parents. Under this plan, we do not send all children of a grade to the store to buy the same book. We tell them to wait until we tell them what to buy or we have them all hand in their "book-money" and use it to buy the right books later.

This system is in direct contrast with the usual one of giving all the children in a room the same book and expecting the poor readers to go more slowly. When, as is often the case, the slow section is a whole grade lower in reading ability, the children in it certainly do go more slowly but they improve their reading very little in the process. They keep meeting too many strange words. They find sentences too long. They are reduced to a guessing, stumbling process that is the opposite of good reading. Reading must be thought getting with incidental word learning, and such a process is impossible unless the reading is easy enough. It is ridiculous to give the same book to groups of children who are a grade or more apart in reading ability. Such a practice rapidly produces remedial reading cases. Different books for different groups is such an easy way of prevention that it can be adopted anywhere with immediate good results.

C. Above the primary grades, the rapid reading period may be a preventive measure.

Above grade three, we should still have in each room a section of poor readers reading material of their own low reading grade, but it may be impossible or difficult to do this. In that case, the establishment of a rapid reading period may prevent the turning of poor readers against all reading and thus stopping their progress. In the ordinary reading period these children may be compelled to get what they can from listening. But when the time for rapid reading comes, each pupil can get an easy book, of about the level at which he is really reading, and can continue his pleasant experiences with reading. He will learn new words because there are bound to be enough of these in any book he takes up. He will continue to speed up his eye movements because he can read the easy book rapidly and he will develop still further his span of attention and his comprehension. The first three grades may have preserved reading as an interesting subject and may have kept the child improving at his own slow rate. If that method has to be abandoned at grade four, the rapid reading period will do something to prevent development of wrong attitudes and an arrest of progress.

For the rapid reading period, each room should be provided with a "room library," consisting of at least a hundred books, ranging in reading difficulty from two grades lower than the room itself to one grade higher. A hundred books is a very small number, being only three books per child, but teachers can help the situation by exchanging books from room to room and by borrowing books from the public library. Every year at least a dollar per child should be appropriated for books for the room library to replace worn out books and to increase the supply. Be glad that books are worn out as that is proof that they are used. And books are used most if in room libraries, where the teacher can see that each child reads as much of the right kind of books as is possible.

D. In junior and senior high school, some of the uniform requirements may be altered.

In the junior and senior high school, poor readers have been helped a great deal by allowing them to take courses suited to their abilities. Yet, in the English work, which is required of all, there is usually an inflexible course of study which demands the same reading of all students regardless of their reading ability. Part of the situation is caused by the common use of anthologies which, being designed for the average student of the average school (an average hoped for rather than actually found) are far out of reach of poor readers.

Something has been done by permitting poor readers to do their outside reading in books suited to grades considerably below high school level. For this purpose, high school libraries should be well supplied with such books or the principal should see that nearby public libraries have plenty of them. However the problem of the "classics" with the poor reader is still unsolved. Practically all the works commonly used are suitable for reading only by students of more than average ability. One solution is gradually to lessen the number of classics or to find those which make easier reading. Another solution is frankly to present the classics to be heard rather than read. In the case of poetry the teacher or the good readers can present the material for the enjoyment of all. Parts of the prose may be presented in the same way. Or when these changes are not made in the work, poor readers can be graded more on their composition work and on their general improvement and less on their knowledge of classics and literary history. This altering of the usual procedures can be frankly undertaken as a measure to prevent failure in high school English since failure would have the disasterous effect of turning the children against reading matter and thus lessening the chance that they will ever do any reading after school days are over.[1]

IV. Preventive measures pay.

Schools thrive on the support of parents. The parents of every remedial case are dissatisfied patrons. To some degree, at least, they blame the school for their child's failure. To lessen the number of remedial cases means to gain the support of many of these parents. Such a result is worth much time and effort, and it is worth some expense on the part of the board of education.

Poor readers are a constant drain upon a teacher's time and nervous energy. They wear down the enthusiasm which

---

[1] Special sections for poor readers are discussed on pages 106 to 108.

she should have to be a good teacher for all her children. The behavior of defense and retaliation which is common with poor readers may cripple any teacher's effectiveness no matter how able she may be. All of this is waste and loss. Any preventive measures which will save some of this "teacher power" will pay big dividends to the whole system.

Failure in reading is likely to mean failure in the child's whole educational life. It means a shortening of schooling. It means going into work of a lower level. It means wrong attitudes of many kinds. It often definitely means development of poor citizenship. Any measures which may prevent some of this social loss will certainly pay to a degree too great to be measured.

SOME USEFUL BOOKS

The following books contain many suggestions for Remedial Reading which will be of value to the teacher. The comment upon each is merely to suggest its scope. The professional library of any school can well include all of these books.

GATES, ARTHUR I.: *The Improvement of Reading*, McMillan & Company, New York, 1935.

A complete report of the researches of the author and his students up to time of publication. Also includes the most significant work of others. Special chapters on remedial instruction for handicapped and for non-readers. Detailed description of eight typical cases of reading disability.

BETTS, EMMETT, ALBERT: *The Prevention and Correction of Reading Difficulties*, Row, Peterson & Company, Evanston, Illinois, 1936.

An excellent compilation of materials on this subject from many sources. An easy book to use because of chapter summaries. The bibliographies are complete up to date of publication. Complete description and directions are given for use of the telebinocular.

MONROE, MARION, AND BACKUS, BERTIE: *Remedial Reading,* Houghton-Mifflin, Boston, 1937.

A full description of a city remedial reading campaign. Contains a very complete analysis of factors in reading disability and a description of use of the Marion Monroe method for correction.

The Thirty-sixth Year Book of the National Society for the Teaching of Education, Part One, *The Teaching of Reading,* Public School Publishing Company, Bloomington, Illinois, 1936.

Many chapters in this report have reference to remedial reading. Chapter 13, entitled ''Diagnosis and Treatment of Extreme Cases of Reading Disability'' is a summary of much work in the field.

COLE, LUELLA: *The Improvement of Reading,* Farrar & Rinehart, New York, 1938.

A book full of practical suggestions. Shows sympathetic understandings of children. Of special value for those who believe in special devices and exercises.

RUSSELL, D. H., KARP, ETTA E., AND KELLY, EDWARD L.: *Reading Aids Through the Grades,* (225 Remedial reading activities), Bureau of Publications, Teachers College, Columbia University, New York, 1938.

Devices copied from all possible sources. Actually devices for teaching and testing reading rather than ones with special remedial purpose.

TRAXLER, ARTHUR E.: *The Teaching of Corrective Reading in the Junior High School,* Public School Publishing Company, Bloomington, Illinois.

This pamphlet is packed with sound and practical suggestions for work with poor readers. It deals especially with group work.

McCALLISTER, J. M.: *Remedial and Corrective Instruction in Reading,* (A Program for Upper Grades and High School), D. Appleton, Century & Company, New York, 1936.

A compilation from many sources. Full descriptions of corrective programs by the author. Most valuable for one who has some experience with remedial work.

CENTER, STELLA S., AND PERSONS, GLADYS: *Teaching High School Students to Read,* D. Appleton, Century & Company, New York, 1937.

Report of a project in remedial instruction in New York High School. Interesting study of many kinds of difficulty and types of students.

WITTY, PAUL, AND KOPEL, DAVID: *Reading and the Educative Process,* Ginn & Company, Boston, 1939.

A careful compilation, intended for college classes, of all the research in the field of remedial reading, with complete data and bibliographies. A valuable reference book.

DOLCH, E. W.: *The Psychology and Teaching of Reading,* Ginn & Company, Boston, 1931.

Since remedial reading is essentially reteaching reading, the teacher should have a clear understanding of what the reading process is. This book presents the matter in simple, non-technical, understandable form.

APPENDIX A

TEACHER'S READING CASE REPORT

Reading Case..By..Date

I. The child's physical condition.
   - A. In what condition are the child's eyes?
     1. Need correction for vision or astigmatism?
     2. Work together correctly?
     3. Is there eye fatigue?
   - B. The state of hearing?
   - C. Speech defect?
   - D. Left-handedness?
   - E. General health?
   - F. Past sickness record?

II. Aspects of the child's school life.
   - A. Does the pupil like school?
   - B. What school subjects does he like?
   - C. Is he good at playground activities or other extra-curricular work?
   - D. Does he play freely and as an equal with the children of his grade?
   - E. How many non-promotions has the child had and when, and why?

III. Aspects of the child's home life.
   - A. Does he coöperate happily with his parents?
   - B. Ages, grade placement, and school success of his brothers and sisters.
   - C. What home hobbies does he have?
   - D. What does he want to be when he grows up?
   - E. Does he work after school hours and at what?

IV. Facts about the child's reading.
   - A. Grade level of the books he reads easily?
   - B. Does he know common words easily by sight?
   - C. Does he miscall words and read right on, or does he correct his mistakes?
   - D. Does he try to sound out new words, and if so, with what success?
   - E. How well does he comprehend easy material?

APPENDIX B

A BASIC SIGHT VOCABULARY OF 220 WORDS

E. W. DOLCH

Since these two hundred and twenty words make up from 50 per cent to 75 per cent of all ordinary reading matter, they should be recognized instantly by sight by all school children. Teaching of these words is described on page 54.

a	come	had	many	round	together
about	could	has	may	run	too
after	cut	have	me		try
again		he	much	said	two
all	did	help	must	saw	
always	do	her	my	say	under
am	does	here	myself	see	up
an	done	him		seven	upon
and	don't	his		shall	us
any	down	hold	never	she	use
are	draw	hot	new	show	
around	drink	how	no	sing	very
as		hurt	not	sit	
ask	eat		now	six	walk
at	eight	I		sleep	want
ate	every	if	of	small	warm
away		in	old	so	was
	fall	into	on	some	wash
be	far	is	once	soon	we
because	fast	it	one	start	well
been	find	its	only	stop	went
before	first		open		were
best	five	jump	or	take	what
better	fly	just	our	tell	when
big	for		out	ten	where
black	found	keep	over	thank	which
blue	four	kind	own	that	white
both	from	know		the	who
bring	full		pick	their	why
brown	funny	laugh	play	them	will
but	gave	let	please	then	wish
buy	get	light	pretty	there	with
by	give	like	pull	these	work
	go	little	put	they	would
call	goes	live		think	write
came	going	long	ran	this	
can	good	look	read	those	yellow
carry	got		red	three	yes
clean	green	made	ride	to	you
cold	grow	make	right	today	your

[154]

APPENDIX C

INSTRUCTIONS FOR THE BASIC SIGHT VOCABULARY CARDS

These 220 words make up 50 to 75 per cent of all school reading matter. They are recognized instantly by good second grade readers and by average third grade readers. The first step in remedial reading is to see that the child recognizes these words instantly by sight.

CHECKING THE PUPIL'S SIGHT KNOWLEDGE

1. Make this a game. Insist it doesn't matter how many are right or wrong. Quiet nervousness. Take time to talk to the child and put him at his ease.

2. Sight words should be "one-look" words. That is, the child should recognize them instantly, without hesitation.

3. Check the child's sight knowledge of these words by the following procedure:

a. If the child is timid, and you do not expect him to know very many words, hand him the pack and tell him you just want him to look through them to see if he knows any of them. Tell him to put them down, one at a time and just put in a separate pile any that he happens to know. Do not urge speed.

b. If the child is confident, put the pack of cards before him at reading distance. Be sure to have the easiest words on the top.

c. Tell the pupil the game is to call the word just as soon as he sees it, giving it only one look. It doesn't matter whether he gets them right or wrong. You just want to separate the "one-look" words from the "two-look" words. He is to tell you which are the "two-look" words if you do not notice.

d. Then sit at the child's right hand and start shifting the cards off the top of the pack. Do this slowly and steadily, at the rate of about one card every second.

e. When a child calls a word correctly, put the card in one stack; when he calls it incorrectly, put it in another. If he does not call it, do not pause but put it in the "two-look" stack. Don't make corrections. You can tell in nearly every case whether the child uses "one-look" or "two-looks." There will be self-correction, wrong calling, or delay.

[155]

f. If the child is to use the particular stack of cards, it is sufficient just to keep the two piles of known and unknown apart by rubber bands. If the child is not to use the cards as a matter of record list the unknown words if they are the largest group. If not, list the known.

g. Watch for *reversals*. Whole words may be reversed or wrong words will be called that are obviously suggested by the end of the word looked at. This is very important, as it helps explain why the child has not learned sight vocabulary.

h. Notice whether a child attempts to sound out words. Does he attack the more common words or the less usual? What success does he have?

i. Watch to see if the child definitely knows the words he calls correctly or if he is more or less guessing at them. These two conditions show different kinds of word perception.

Caution. Study the individual case. Some children naturally react quickly and some slowly. Some are careless and some not. "Instant recognition" may be a little different for different ones. Vary the procedure to fit the case.

TEACHING THE SIGHT VOCABULARY

1. The purpose is to have all of these 220 words recognized instantly, without a second glance. When the child can so recognize them, he will instantly recognize more than half the words he meets in reading, will have renewed confidence, and will be able to devote his attention to the other words of the reading matter and to the thought it expresses.

2. If the pupil knows only a few of the words at the start, he should be given a pack made up of those words and about an equal number of new ones. When he has learned the new ones, he should have other new ones added to his pack. The idea is that he should have a mixture of known and unknown, without too many unknown, but with enough known ones to keep him feeling confident.

3. If the pupil knows half or more of the words, give him the whole pack. Put them in an envelope, bearing his name and marked on the outside with a series of numbers, to represent his successive practices with the cards.

4. As soon as the pupil knows more than half of the cards, provide him with a "helper" who is a good reader who knows all the words. Call the remedial pupil a "player."

5. Every day (or sometimes twice a day) have the player shuffle his cards, and then go over them rapidly, saying each word and handing the card to the helper. If the player gets the word right, the helper keeps the card. If the player gets it wrong or cannot say the word, the helper puts the card on a pile on the desk. This method of handling prevents confusion. Then the cards on which help is needed are counted, and the number entered after the number of the practice on the outside of the envelope.

6. The pack of unknown cards should then be gone over, the helper telling each word as the player looks at it, and the player repeating the word after him. These cards are then shuffled back into the pack ready for the next practice.

7. The record on the outside of the envelope is to show the teacher and the pupil the progress made.

8. The unknown are mixed with the known so that the pupil will develop rapid calling of the words. If all the unknown are together, the habit of slow calling will be developed.

9. Practice is continued until the player can call all the words, instantly, for at least three consecutive practices.

CAUTIONS

1. This learning must be a game, not a punishment. Praise must be used continually.

2. "Helpers" must be chosen wisely. They must be agreeable to the learner, tactful, and not puffed up, and must understand that the player is to call the words after "one-look" but that the player himself is supposed to coöperate in telling when more than one look was required.

3. It will be understood, of course, that if the teacher were helping the child she would point out prominent word characteristics and make word comparisons, but pupil helpers cannot be expected to do this. They can only tell the learner the word, the latter learning it by sheer repeated seeing and saying.

APPENDIX D

SPEECH SURVEY

(Prepared by Dr. Severina Nelson, Department of Speech, University of Illinois, to be used by the teacher as a general check on the more common speech difficulties in her class.)

Name..Address..

School..Grade................Telephone No..............

1. Indistinct Speech:

Dialects..

Foreign Accent...............................

Lisping..

Poor Enunciation...........................

Deficient Sounds:

a (bait)............ o (coat)...........

a (bat)............ oo (pool)...........

a (above)......... oo (look)...........

a (father)........ ou (house)..........

aw (law)..............ow (how)............

b (bib)............ oy (boy)............

c as k (cook)........... p (pup)............

ch (church)........ r (rear)............

d (deed)........... s (cease)..........

e (beet)............s as z (boys)......

e (bet)..............sh (mission)......

f (fife)............ t (toot)...........

g (gag)............. th (third)..........

h (hail)............. th (then)..........

i (ice).............. u (use)............

i (it)............... u (pull)...........

j (judge)......... v (value)..........

l (lull)............. w (wail)...........

m (maim).........wh (whale)..........

n (noon)........... y (young)........

ng (sing)........... z (zones)..........

2. Unpleasant Voice:

Nasality......................................

Monotone....................................

High Pitch...................................

Hoarseness...................................

Huskiness.....................................

Throatiness..................................

Any unusual
voice quality...............................

3. Stuttering or stammering.........

Remarks.......................................

....

....

....

....

Suggested Therapy:......................

....

....

....

....

....

....

....

Examiner............................

APPENDIX E

THE OPHTHALMOGRAPH AND THE
METRONOSCOPE

PHOTOGRAPHING EYE MOVEMENTS

For many years, laboratories which studied reading problems have photographed eye movements. The machine used contained the usual 35 mm motion-picture film which moved at a constant rate behind a pair of lenses. Each lense focused upon the film spots of light reflected from the readers eyeballs and which were cast on the eye by a light shining through a small hole in a box which contained an electric bulb. Every movement of the pair of eyes was recorded upon the film by the movement of the spots of light reflected from the eyeballs. The standard procedure was to ask the subject to read five or six lines on a card placed at the proper reading distance and thus to secure on the film a record of the eye movements during this reading.

The purpose of photographing the eye movements has been to study what were called "reading habits." It was assumed that the eyes of each individual moved in certain habitual ways during reading. If then a record of the eyes' habitual movements could be secured, it was assumed that remedial exercises could be given to change these habits.

There has now been put on the market a very compact and effective machine for making eye movement photographs. Reading clinics everywhere have these machines and they are also found in the offices of school psychologists and others interested in the problems of poor readers. Many schools are wondering whether they should possess one of these machines or, if they have one, how they should use it.

First of all, it must be said that no one should imagine, when he has secured an eye movement photograph for a child that he has fully adequate material for a diagnosis of that child's reading difficulties. The eye movement photograph tells what the child's eyes did in reading a certain short selection at a certain time. It does not tell what the child's eyes do in reading at all times. Two variables must be always kept in mind. (1) The child's reading changes as the material changes. The protograph shows the reading of a certain test card. Suppose an easier card had been used, or a harder one. It is easily shown in the photographing of the eye movement that we can change the record on the film in many ways by changing the material that the child is asked to read. This does not mean that the child does not have eye movement habits. Instead it shows either that he has various habits or that his habits change with changing conditions. (2) The other variable is the child's purpose, we find that we can change the record on the film by telling the child to read rapidly or to read very carefully or in some other special way. The standard directions for photographing eye movements are: You should read as rapidly as you can, remembering that you will answer a few questions about what you have read. It has been found that the direction ''read rapidly'' registers strongly with some children and causes them to hurry more than usual; while the warning about a ''few questions'' registers with others and causes them to slow down.

These two limitations of the photograph secured by use of the machine are very important when we think of the kind of reading we are going to have the remedial case do. We are not going to have him read these standard cards with these standard directions. We are going to give him school books and other books of various degrees of difficulty and of interest for him. We are going to give him many purposes in reading and ask him all sorts of questions. Therefore, the eye movement photograph showing reading of a certain piece of text, following certain directions, is a *sample* of the child's eye movement. It is a *special* sample which must be taken as such. It is valuable if one remembers exactly the card the child was reading and the exact conditions which surrounded that reading. The photograph is valuable especially to a person who has personally taught many remedial cases how to read. Such a person understands how the child's mind works and what effects him and how. As a part of this total understanding of the remedial process, the sample given by the photograph is helpful. But a study of eye movement photographs, apart from the child's total situation, is definitely misleading and may be clearly harmful. The concept that the child has a single reading habit, supposed to be very like a habit of handwriting, leads to mechanical exercises which may not at all fit the whole complicated situation. Such a partial and distorted view of the use of eye movement photographs is by all means to be avoided.

Second, we wish to point out that eye movement photographs need to be interpreted in detail. Common practice is to count the forward movements, count the regressive movements, and give averages, including fixations per 100 words, regressions per 100 words, duration of fixations per 100 words, number of words per fixation, and number of words per minute. These averages may or may not be very significant depending upon how uniform the child's performance was during the reading of the lines. But in a reading case the chances are against uniform performance. One line may consist of familar words and may be read with ease. Another line may contain an unknown word which causes great confusion, with many regressions, long fixations, or a mere wavering of the eyes back and forth. And still another line may contain an unfamiliar idea which causes a mental confusion which shows itself in hesitating and confused eye movements. Therefore, to interpret a strip of film showing the reading of a number of lines of print, one must lay down beside the film the card which was read and compare the two line by line to try to discover the causes for the many kinds of movement which the film shows. While doing this one must remember the question raised above, whether the particular card was probably easy for the child to read, hard for him to read, contained certain unknown words or the like. It is in this interpretation of eye movement records that there has been the greatest failure to make proper use of them.

Third, we must call attention to the check on comprehension which accompanies the usual photographing of eye movements. The standard procedure gives ten statements on the back of each card which is read. Immediately after the photographing, these statements are read to the child, and he answers "yes" or "no" depending on whether the statements agree with the paragraph just read. Thus the check on comprehension is planned to be immediate memory as determined by true or false statements. The percentage of statements which the pupil gets right is called his comprehension score.

Several comments need to be made concerning this comprehension score. First, it is obvious that mere chance would give on the average a comprehension score of 50 per cent. This fact is keenly appreciated by all workers in education who use true and false or yes-no tests. It must not be forgotten here. Second, we must point out that many of the questions can be answered from previous knowledge. This has been found to be an especial difficulty with some of the cards which deal with facts in history. It is to some extent a difficulty with all the cards because about half of the statements are always false, and common sense or general experience will often detect falsity even without the reading of the cards. Third, it is found that the child, when first photographed, generally paid so much attention to the unusual experience that he was not trying hard enough to remember details. But after having tried to answer ten questions on one card he will be more cautious next time in his reading and therefore be able to answer more questions. We should know, therefore, whether an eye movement photograph is the first one made or whether it had been preceded by others. Finally, we must raise the question whether the kind of reading in which a child tries to remember ten details from six lines of text is the kind we are trying to teach in remedial reading. This is really part of the question which we raised in the last section, whether the type of reading done with the eye photographing machine is typical of the type of reading we are planning on teaching.

THE METRONOSCOPE

Many schools are wondering whether they should own as part of their equipment a metronoscope. This is a machine which is essentially an automatic flashing device. The machine, which is placed in front of the classroom, is a metal box on a stand. This box contains a roll on which is printed in large type, similar to that used on flash cards, a continuous story or article. One line of the story, containing from four to seven words according to grade level, appears at a time in a long window across the front of the machine. A motor can be set to show one line after another in this window at different rates per minute, or the teacher can, by hand, change from one line to the next. By setting the machine at a certain number of lines per minute, a definite speed of reading can be established, and the children must read at this speed if they are to keep up with the story. Thus, used line by line, the machine is a "pushing device," very similar to the use of a card described on page 80 except that when a card is used the child can read ahead, whereas when the machine is used the child may read to the end of the line and then have to wait until the next line appears.

Another feature of the flashing machine is that automatically operated shutters may be switched on so that only a third of the line is shown at one time. When these shutters are used, the left third opens and shuts, the center third opens and shuts and the right third opens and shuts. The roll behind the shutter is so printed that each time entire words appear and not parts of words. The purpose of these shutters is to control the reader's eye movements. The reader must go from left to right. Then many persons who use the machine believe that the reader is expected to see with one fixation what is exposed by each shutter. Such a result would mean three fixations a line and that small number of fixations is not found in the photographic records which we have even of very good readers. Therefore, what really happens is that the reader makes several fixations for each opening of a shutter.

How does this machine work in remedial reading? There are various published reports but they all say that the operators followed the prescribed procedure and they then give the results in terms of average fixations per line, average number of regressions, etc. Such results do not tell how different types of children, at different grade levels, with different kinds of reading difficulties, react to the use of the machine. We have shown that success in remedial reading depends on adaptation of all methods and material to the great variations found in individual cases. We must point, therefore, how the use of the metronoscope must be adapted to individual cases.

The *first* caution in the use of the metronoscope is not to scare the child. The poor reader is nearly always timid, or afraid that he will fail at any task involving reading. To put him, without preparation, before this machine with its snapping shutters may cause a reaction of fear that will make all further use of the machine useless. Therefore, the best approach is to show the child how the whole thing works or even let him put the roll into the machine. He should see it operate without any requirement of reading. Then the reading of the material must be approached gradually as a game. Each story on a roll is preceded by a list of hard words selected from the story. The idea is to make sure that the child can recognize these words before the story is shown. Plenty of time must be taken for this word list. The teacher will have to turn from one line to the next by hand. To some children the words will be taught as sight words, the child being told the word and asked to repeat it. In some cases the child may be encouraged to work out the word himself, depending upon the place of sounding in his remedial program. When the reading of the story is begun, it is important to begin very slowly so that some confidence is developed. Above all the child must like his work with the machine and want to continue with it.

Second, this flashing machine has a distinct value as a motivating device with older children who have become very antagonistic toward reading. Older boys, especially, are fascinated by the mechanics of the thing. It gets and holds their attention in a way that usual reading materials cannot. If the machine is introduced correctly, this same motivating effect ought to result with all types of remedial cases.

Third, beginning work with the metronoscope should be oral reading. This is essential for several reasons. First, it is absolutely necessary to know what the child is doing. Does he really know all of the words? Which words are causing trouble? Is he keeping up with the machine? What does he do if it gets ahead of him? Neglect of these important points may cause the machine to do more harm than good.

Fourth, the child must be taught a technique of responding to the machine. At first a poor reader may come to a word he does not know, becomes confused, look at the teacher, and lose the next two or three lines. Instead he must be taught when he missed a word to pass over it and to pay sharp attention to what follows. In other words, he must be taught to skip and go on. He must do this because the machine will not stop for him. Some children quickly adapt themselves to the way the machine goes on without regard for their doubt or hesitation. Other children become terribly worried and confused. This practically means that some cases cannot use the machine with much profit.

Finally, we come to the greatest problem involved in the use of the metronoscope by schools. It is using the machine to increase speed of reading. The machine is presented to the schools primarily as a device to increase reading speed. Most persons think of it as a device for that purpose. But many problems are involved, which we shall try to indicate, leaving it to further research to determine the final answers.

In the *first* place, no provision is made by this automatic flashing machine for the meeting of strange words. It is true, each story is preceded by a list of words to be taught before the reading begins, but these lists include more words than any child can be taught at one sitting. Then it is inevitable that, in the reading, other strange words appear, since no one can predict exactly which will be the hard words for a particular child. Thus on practically every use of the metronoscope the child is sure to encounter words which he does not recognize and which he cannot stop to figure out because the machine goes ahead at its fixed rate. As we have mentioned above, the child must be taught the method of letting the unknown word go and paying close attention to what comes next. The result is naturally what may be called "reading with gaps." Using the machine to increase speed of reading means getting speed by teaching the habit of skipping unknown words in this way. This kind of speed may be desirable for some kinds of reading, but it is undesirable for others. Some children need this kind of reading developed because they spend too much time puzzling over difficult words and do not go on to get what they can from the whole text. Other children need to be strongly discouraged from skipping hard words because they use that method at all times instead of trying to work out strange words when they should. Therefore, the way in which the metronoscope secures speed is not desirable at all times and with all children.

In the *second* place, using this machine to increase speed of reading raises the question of the degree of comprehension. The directions which come with the machine say that a roll should be run too fast for a child to "get it all." In fact, they say that a roll should be run five or six times before the comprehension is complete. Now it is obvious that if we compel a reader to hurry over some material he is bound to get less out of it. These directions which say complete comprehension requires five or six readings of the same roll certainly contemplate a great deal of hurrying. Here is a very fundamental query regarding speed of reading. Do we want speed at the expense of comprehension? One answer is that a little increase in speed may not materially effect amount of comprehension. Makers of the metronoscope claim that they have proven this to be true because a child may go faster than usual in reading a roll and still answer perfectly the questions at the end of the roll. But these questions do not cover all the material on the roll, they call chiefly for mere memory, and, being a new type, they can often be answered from general information. A second answer often given is that large gain in speed off-sets the small loss in comprehension which results. These might be true if the loss in comprehension were small, but the poorer the reader the greater this loss is. The child who is getting little from his reading when given his usual time will get practically nothing if pushed more than a very little at a time. In short, the relation of comprehension to the speeding up process recommended with the metronoscope must be studied more carefully than it is at present.

Finally, we have with the metronoscope the usual problem of transfer. If the child reads under controlled conditions with the machine for a short period each day, will he use the same method in all the other reading he does? There is as yet no answer to this question. In all probability the transfer to all reading will depend upon the child's conscious effort to practice all of the time what he has been taught in the reading period.

Group use of the metronoscope is a matter somewhat different from what we have so far been discussing. With a group, complete adaptation to all individuals is impossible. For instance, some may be frightened and some entirely confident. What will be a hard word for one will not be for another. Present speeds of reading will all be different. Degrees of comprehension will all be different. Therefore, the best that can be done with a group is to approximate what most of them need. Most may be helped but some will not be. Therefore, it is important that each member be watched carefully and any individual who is not getting along be removed. He had better not be in the class at all if he is not being helped, for there is always the likelihood that he may be really harmed.

There still remains a very recent move to use the metronoscope in regular primary teaching. Here we must re-emphasize that it is merely a flash card machine. It can probably flash cards as well as the teacher except that the teacher holds the cards before her and can perhaps get better attention than a machine which stands in a fixed position. The rolls which have been provided do contain a great deal of material which the average primary teacher does not have available. But similar material could be available in card form. In short, use of a machine to do flashing in primary grades depends upon whether the flashing method is to be extensively used and then on whether the teacher prefers to use the machine or to flash by other methods.

Date Due